Lord, What Should I Do?

by Fred R. Coulter

For the cover:
Graphics by Curley Creative
Photograph by Ken Pratt

All Scriptural references and quotes are from
The Holy Bible In Its Original Order—
A Faithful Version with Commentary,
Second Edition 2009, 2010, 2011
York Publishing Company.
ISBN 978-0-9819787-0-3

ISBN 978-0-9819787-6-5
© 2011
Second Printing 2015
York Publishing Company
Post Office Box 1038
Hollister, CA 95024-1038

www.cbcg.org
www.churchathome.org
www.theoriginalbiblerestored.org
www.afaithfulversion.org
www.iglesiadedioscristianaybiblica.org

Contents

About the Author

Fred R. Coulter attended the University of San Francisco and graduated from San Mateo State College before graduating from Ambassador University (Ambassador College), Pasadena, California, with a BA in Theology in 1964. He was ordained a minister of Jesus Christ in 1965 and pastored churches of God in the Pacific Northwest, the Mountain States, the greater Los Angeles area and Monterey, including the central coast area of California. Mr. Coulter completed advanced biblical and ministerial studies in 1972-75 under the Ambassador University Master's Program. While completing these studies, he was encouraged by his professor of *Koiné* Greek to consider translating the books of the New Testament.

For the next twenty years, Mr. Coulter diligently studied, continuing to expand his knowledge of *Koiné* Greek. While undertaking a verse-by-verse study of the books of the New Testament, he was moved to translate the New Testament into clear, easy-to-read English for contemporary readers—resulting in *The New Testament In Its Original Order* (now incorporated into *The Holy Bible In Its Original Order—A Faithful Version With Commentary*).

Fred Coulter has dedicated his life and talents to restoring original Christianity for today's generation. Laying aside all traditions of men, he has preached the truth of the Scriptures as taught by Jesus Christ and the apostles—proclaiming Jesus as personal Savior for all. Since 1983, Mr. Coulter has been the president of the Christian Biblical Church of God, headquartered in Hollister, California. He has an active ministry which reaches all parts of the United States and Canada, with additional offices in Australia, New Zealand, the United Kingdom, South Africa, Ethiopia and Kenya.

Each year over 1,200,000 people from around the world actively utilize the church's Web sites where they find timely, inspiring weekly sermons and in-depth verse-by-verse biblical study materials covering virtually all of Scripture (see www.cbcg.org and www.churchathome.org and www.theoriginalbiblerestored.org and www.afaithfulversion.org).

With a ministry now spanning 55 years, Fred Coulter is on a God-inspired mission to preserve the truth of God—*restoring original Christianity for today*—for the next generation of faithful Christians. With today's Christianity experiencing rampant doctrinal confusion, an overall watering down of the truth, and virtual disintegration, Mr. Coulter has been inspired to write *Lord, What Should I Do?* as a practical guide for believers who are determined to find God in a godless society.

Other Works by the Author

The Holy Bible In Its Original Order—A Faithful Version With Commentary is a new translation that reflects the meaning of the original Hebrew and Greek with fidelity and accuracy—and is the only English version in which the books of the Bible are arranged in their original order. The easy-to-read translation retains the grace and grandeur of the *King James Version* while clarifying many of its problematic passages. Included are commentaries on the writing, canonization and preservation of the Scriptures. Various appendices cover numerous controversial biblical teachings, and detailed footnotes and marginal references explain hard-to-understand passages. A vital tool for all students of the Bible!

A Harmony of the Gospels in Modern English brings to life the message and purpose of the true Jesus, portraying His life and ministry in their true historical setting. This easy-to-understand, step-by-step account of the life of Christ is an indispensable study aid for every Bible student.

The Christian Passover details the scriptural and historical truths of the Passover in both the Old and New Testaments, leading the reader step-by-step through every aspect of one of the most vital and fundamental teachings revealed in the Bible. With over 500 pages, the book fully explains the meaning of the Christian Passover—a remembrance of the sacrifice of Jesus Christ, the Passover Lamb of God—in a most compelling and inspiring manner. The full meaning of the body and blood of Jesus Christ is revealed, showing the magnitude of God's love for every person.

The Day Jesus the Christ Died—the Biblical Truth about His Passion, Crucifixion and Resurrection is the *only book* to present "the rest of the story"—left out by Mel Gibson in his epic movie "The Passion of the Christ." Without the true historical and biblical facts, one cannot fully understand the meaning of Jesus Christ's horrific, humiliating and gruesome death by beating, scourging and crucifixion. The author presents the full biblical account in a most compelling way. As you will see, the truth is more astounding than all of the ideas, superstitions and traditions of men!

The Seven General Epistles is designed for an in-depth verse-by-verse study of the epistles of James; I and II Peter; I, II and III John and Jude. As part of the living Word of God, these epistles are as meaningful today for personal Christian growth as when they were written.

Occult Holidays or God's Holy Days—Which? For centuries the leaders of Orthodox Christendom have sold popular holidays—Halloween, Christmas, Easter, etc.—to the masses as though they had "Christian" meaning. This book effectively demonstrates that these celebrated holidays are not of God, but originated from ancient religions rooted in occultism. Contrary to the false ideas of men, the true biblical holy days of God have vital spiritual meaning and outline God's fantastic plan of salvation for all mankind.

God's Plan for Mankind Revealed by His Sabbath and Holy Days.
This first-of-its-kind, 598-page work provides a comprehensive look at
God's amazing Master Plan for the human family—precisely as it is outlined by the biblical seventh-day Sabbath and annual holy days. Each chapter is a transcript of an in-depth sermon or Bible study revealing God's purpose from Genesis to Revelation. Actual sermons are included on an accom-
panying set of four CDs.

The Appointed Times of Jesus the Messiah. Mainstream Christianity has little or no understanding of how Jesus' messianic role has been carefully organized according to what Scripture calls God's "appointed times."
As this book demonstrates, the "appointed times" of the Messiah follow the
timeframe set by the biblical *festivals* and *holy days* as well as the *70-week
prophecy* of Daniel nine—all of which outline God's plan of salvation. Indeed, it is only within this unique context that the role of Jesus as the Messiah can be rightly understood.

Online Studies for the serious Bible student—with additional written material and in-depth Bible studies in audio and video format—can be
obtained at **www.cbcg.org** and **www.churchathome.org**.

Other Authors

Judaism—Revelation of Moses or Religion of Men? Contrary to
Jewish claims, the religion of Judaism—with its elaborate code of traditions—does not represent the way of life God gave through Moses in the
Old Testament. Using history, Scripture and the Jews' own writings, this
book demonstrates that Judaism is actually a false religion developed by
men. *Written by Philip Neal.*

***America and Britain—Their Biblical Origin and Prophetic Des-
tiny.*** The Bible mentions all the great ancient empires: Egypt, Assyria,
Babylon, Medo-Persia, Greece, Rome. But what about the *greatest empire*
in history, the British Empire? What about the most powerful nation in all of
history, the United States? Their *apparent absence* from the Bible has long
puzzled scholars. As this book shows, these great nations are, in fact, dis-
cussed in numerous passages of the Bible—where they are identified by
their *ancient, ancestral names*. Utilizing Scripture and documented history,
the author shows just who the British and American peoples *really are*—
revealing both their biblical origin and astounding prophetic destiny! *Written by Philip Neal.*

Acknowledgments

We first acknowledge God the Father and Jesus Christ, and thank them for preserving the Holy Bible—in spite of mankind's tumultuous history—so that today the truth is available for everyone. It is the very Word of God that gives us the true understanding of the purpose of human existence. Jesus said, "Your Word is the truth" (John 17:17), and "you shall know the truth, and the truth shall set you free" (John 8:32).

A special "thank you" goes to all the faithful brethren whose tithes and offerings made this book possible.

As with my other publications, many people have helped and shared in the production of this book. Their diligent work and support has made it possible. First, I give my heartfelt gratitude and appreciation to my loving, dear wife, Dolores, for her personal encouragement and assistance. Special thanks go to Philip Neal for his research, content contribution and editing, and to John and Hiedi Vogele for proofreading and the final formatting of the text.

Fred R. Coulter
2011, 2015

Introduction

For the past several decades, American mainstream Christianity has been undergoing significant *change*. Many churchgoers are troubled and bewildered by what they see—commercialization, political infighting, corruption and abuse, watered-down doctrines, ineffectiveness. Increasingly, the corporate church is seen as *irrelevant* in today's complex world. Moreover, young people in particularly are *turning away* from church in record numbers.

Why is this? What is happening in our churches?

In her book *Quitting Church*, Julia Duin argues that "**something is not right with church life**" **today**. She says that modern churchgoers are increasingly disappointed by what they consider to be a lack of genuine spirituality. "The problem seems to be the church itself.... [People] have given up on the *institution*" (p. 18). Duin argues that organized religion has become dysfunctional, that its role in the lives of believers lacks focus. Today's church seems focused on *culture*—fads, creative marketing and "packaging." Worship services often border on *entertainment*. Then there are the turf battles, splits and schisms—and the liberalized teachings. While many churchgoers are oblivious to what's happening in the mainstream church, Duin writes that there are those Christians who simply want a "return to a faith that is authentic, relevant and applicable" to modern life (p. 20). Meanwhile, there is a steady decline in church attendance. Churchgoers are beginning to look elsewhere—and they are finding God *outside* the church.

In particular, many churchgoers are hungry for *truth*. Instead, they are bored each week with lifeless sermons and watered-down teachings. Dismayed, they watch as the truth of the Bible is slowly but surely subverted. American churchgoers are now facing what the church in England has long been subject to—*liberalism*. Back in 1993, *The Prophetic Observer*, a fundamentalist evangelical publication, warned of this growing trend:

> "The [Protestant] church in America is under attack! The source of this attack is not primarily humanism, secularism, or agnosticism from without, but *liberalism from within*. Liberalism within the church is **eating away at the core of the fundamental doctrines** of the Christian faith. Christianity in America today is facing the same 'downgrade' that the church in England faced 100 years ago in the days of [the renowned evangelist] Charles Spurgeon.
>
> "Spurgeon said: 'We live in perilous times. We are passing through a most eventful period; the Christian world is convulsed; there is a mighty upheaval of the old founda-

tions of faith; a great overhauling of old teaching. The Bible is made to speak today in a language which to our fathers would be an unknown tongue. **Gospel teachings**, the proclamation of which made men fear to sin and dread the thought of eternity, **are being shelved**. Calvary is being robbed of its glory, sin of its horror, and we are said to be evolving into a reign of vigorous and blessed sentimentality, in which heaven and earth, God and man are to become a heap of sensational emotions; but in the process of [this] evolution, is not the power of the gospel weakened? **Are not our chapels emptying?** Is there not growing up among men a greater indifference to the claims of Christ? Are not the theories of evolution retrogressive in their effect upon the age? Where is the fiery zeal for the salvation of men which marked the nonconformity of the past? Where is the noble enthusiasm that made heroes and martyrs for the truth? Where is the force which carried nonconformity forward like a mighty avalanche? Alas, where?'

"If something is not done to stem the tide, the [growing] wave of liberalism will engulf our nation as it did England at the end of the last century" (Published by Southwest Radio Church, Oklahoma City; November 1993; emphasis added).

Indeed, England has been reduced from the leader of the greatest empire in modern times to a nation dying of moral deprivation—because God has been systematically eliminated not only from all public affairs, but *from the church* as well. America, it seems, is not far behind.

Satan the devil—who is busy deceiving the entire world (Rev 12:9) —is quite subtle and clever in his attack against Christianity. Working from *within*, his "ministers" appear as "ministers of righteousness" (II Cor. 11:15). Yet, many teach liberalized (if not outright paganized) doctrines that lull churchgoers into a spiritual stupor.

As a Christian, you need to wake up and take note of what is now taking place within mainstream Christianity. Are you concerned about the spiritual apathy and malaise that seems to have taken root in the church? Is your church *failing* to meet your family's spiritual needs? Are you starving for *real* biblical understanding? Are you wondering, "Where is the love of God?"

If so, this book is for you. *Lord, What Should I Do?* addresses these timely issues, emphasizing how Christians *can* and *must* defend themselves and their families against the forces of evil that would destroy the truth of God. Moreover, this book *points the way* for churchgoers looking for alternatives to the one-size-fits-all corporate church experience.

What Is Happening to Mainstream Christianity?

Church is supposed to be a haven—a place where one can go for respite, nurturing and encouraging fellowship; a place where one can worship God in comfort and peace; a place were one can be inspired, taught the Scriptures, receive answers to life's questions—and even be corrected. But for millions of Americans, attending church is a thing of the past. They are among the growing ranks of church "dropouts"—those who choose to *stay home* rather than waste time and energy on a church that, in their estimation, no longer represents Christ or that has ceased to be relevant in their lives. **This "exodus of desperation" has been a long time in the making—and is accelerating at an alarming pace**.

Currently the religion editor for *The Washington Times*, Julia Duin has spent much of her career researching this very phenomenon: Why do faithful churchgoers *quit* going to church? In her book *Quitting Church*, Duin points out that *many* churchgoers are skipping church. "It's no secret that the percentage of Americans in church on any given Sunday is dropping fast" (p. 11).

How fast? For the past several years, Gallup polls have shown church attendance at around 43 percent. However, according to a survey sponsored by the National Opinion Research Center at the University of Chicago, religious attendance in America *fell* from 41 percent in 1971 to 31 percent in 2002. That's ten percentage points in 30 years.

Studies conducted in 2005 by sociologists suggest the average attendance is much lower, around 18 to 20 percent—*half* of what Gallup polls indicate. One of the researchers, Dave Olson, said in a report published in the April 2006 issue of *Christianity Today* that **significantly *fewer* Americans are actually participating in traditional churchgoing practices**. Moreover, growth measured in terms of new baptisms has slowed dramatically. Duin notes that most so-called church growth is "due to transfers from one church to another" (p. 12). From her perspective, the trend is undeniable: "evangelicals, for a variety of reasons, are heading out of church"— they are abandoning mega-churches for home-based mini-churches (p. 21).

According to an Associated Press report filed by journalist Tom Breen, older mainline Protestant churches across the nation are struggling to maintain their facilities due to shrinking budgets—a natural consequence of *declining membership*. In fact, many churches are *losing* their sanctuaries because they can no longer pay their mortgage debt. Since 2008, nearly 200 religious facilities have been foreclosed on by banks—up from only eight during the previous two years. Some borrowed too much or built too big during boom times and now are under tremendous financial pressure. While rising unemployment and a weak economy are certainly part of the problem, the ongoing drop in church attendance is a major factor. As congregations shrink, so do contributions.

For example, Breen writes that the Metropolitan United Methodist Church in Detroit was completed in 1926; at the time, it was the most expensive Methodist facility ever built. By 1949, it had just over 10,000 members, more than any Methodist congregation in the world. Today, he writes, "membership is at 375, in a city where Methodist churches have *fallen from 77 to 16.*"

Breen says the Detroit Methodist church's decline is "mirrored among Protestant denominations like the Lutherans, Presbyterians and Episcopalians, which have seen memberships drop in recent decades while the average age of remaining worshippers gets older." He quotes Robert Jaeger, executive director of the Partnership for Sacred Places, who says that numerous mainline churches "have shrunk from 500 members to 100 members, or from 800 members to 200 members" (Breen, *Congregations Struggle in Aging, Decaying Churches*, July 17, 2010).

But mainstream denominations are not the only groups facing steep declines in attendance. Even the Sabbatarian Seventh Day Adventist (SDA) movement—with some 15 million members worldwide—is undergoing a mass exodus of unhappy churchgoers. According to the group's own research, SDA membership in the United States alone has dropped some 40 percent over the past two decades—from about 750,000 to 450,000. Worldwide, nearly 1.4 million members left the SDA church from 2000 to 2005. Even worse, only 50 percent of those still "on the rolls" actually attend services. Studies indicate that 80 percent of former Adventists cite "doctrinal issues" as the reason for dropping out (Dr. Pieter Barkhuizen, "Let the Truth Set Us Free," Biblical Research Perspectives; www.scribd.com/doc/22319905/Let-the-Truth-Set-Us-Free-052809).

What's behind all the empty pews? Why are people *quitting* church? Duin estimates that 78 million Protestants are church *dropouts* (p. 20). For them, Sunday mornings at church have become too boring or painful. "People are bored witless at church. Skipping a Sunday doesn't distract from the quality of their week," writes Duin. Why? "Church has nothing to do with their actual lives. **What's preached and talked about is *irrelevant* to their daily existence in the twenty-first century**" (p. 32; emphasis added). Thus, "large groups of Christians are opting out of church because they find it impossible to stay" (p. 21). Moreover, evangelical pollster George Barna, founder of the influential Barna Group, estimates that the number of "unchurched" Americans is growing at the rate of about one million each year (p. 13). But as we will see, these dropouts have not suddenly become irreligious; rather, they are frustrated by the overall *failure* of the established church.

The Increasingly *Irrelevant* Church

A sad commentary on the ability of today's churches to retain members is reflected in the aftermath of 9/11. Immediately following the terrorist attacks, churches became packed, spiking growth charts. Within a few months, however, attendance began dropping sharply as the "seekers" (as Duin calls them) fell away *unimpressed* (p. 13).

As a reporter covering religion in America, Duin writes that she has been amazed to witness the number of people who have dropped out of church. The most common complaint, she notes, was the *banality* of the church (p. 16). Churchgoers are tired of stale, "same old, same old" forms of worship; the spiritual gruel offered Sunday after Sunday has become unpalatable; they are troubled by the ongoing watering down of doctrine; and, they are concerned that many Christians, especially the younger ones, do not take the Bible seriously (particularly on issues such as divorce and premarital sex).

"**The problem seems to be the [organized, established] church itself**. Survey after survey says many Americans continue their private religious practices, such as reading the Bible, praying to God, and even sharing their faith in Jesus Christ. **But they have given up on the institution**" (p. 18; emphasis added). Duin says that many churches today are "seeker-friendly"—where services are kept not only short, but bland enough to ensure that newcomers will not feel pressured or uncomfortable (p. 16). But this does nothing for the Christian who is starving for substantive biblical teaching. For example, one church dropout wrote that "the local church has become its own culture—from mega-churches with creative marketing campaigns to Christian music, Christian books, Christian clothing, and even Christian weight-loss programs. These things, in and of themselves, are well and good—but they are no substitute for a fleshed-out faith" (p. 20; quoted from *Christianity Today*, March 2006).

In his book *Your Jesus Is Too Safe*, Jared Wilson challenges Christians to leave behind their drive-through, feel-good Jesus and embrace the true Christ. He argues that "no message has been more used and exploited and appropriated than Jesus Christ's…. [No] historical figure has been more marginalized and commoditized than Jesus. For many today, He is a generic brand, a logo, a catchphrase, a pick-me-up" (p. 12). A good example is the "WWJD" (What Would Jesus Do?) motto popularized by young churchgoers throughout the 1990s. The WWJD logo is still proudly displayed by thousands of youths on wristbands and bracelets. But how many young people really *know* (or even care) what Jesus *would do* in any given circumstance? Are kids today closer to God as a result of the WWJD marketing fad? As statistics will show, such campaigns are typically ineffective at bringing about real spiritual growth; in fact, *worldliness* continues to make serious inroads into the church, corrupting our youth. The reality is, clever, catchphrase "Jesus marketing" does not change people's lives.

Wilson adds: "It's no wonder the world doesn't *get* Jesus, because we've spent decades selling a Jesus cast in our own image." As a result, our popular Jesus "has inspired millions to say a prayer to get His forgiveness— and then go on living lives devoid of His presence.... **In much of the church today, we worship a *convenient* Jesus. We designate Him as our 'Lord and Savior,' but this phrase tends to serve as merely a label that, in our superficially spiritual lives, belies His real function—our Great Example**" (pp. 13-14; emphasis added). The bottom line is that Christianity's popular bumper-sticker Jesus is just not *relevant* to the real problems and stresses people are facing.

The problem of irrelevancy extends even to a large group of unchurched young adults called *millennials*. According to Thom Rainer, president and CEO of LifeWay Christian Research, millennials—more than 78 million strong—are those born between 1980 and 2000. The group has already surpassed "Baby Boomers" as the larger and more influential generation in America. In his book *The Millennials,* Rainer describes the group as being keenly aware of the failings of Christianity. In particular they note that too many Christians have a "low commitment" to their faith, and they see churches as typically "inward focused"—which turns them off. Rainer's research shows that **an astounding 70 percent of millennials believe the church is one of the "least relevant institutions in society"** (Michelle Vul, *The Christian Post*, Jan. 12, 2011; www.christianpost.com/article/20110112/ few-millenials-interested-in-religion-study-finds/).

LifeWay Research has conducted numerous surveys in an effort to get a handle on why so many churchgoers are opting out of traditional services. Brad Waggoner, director of the organization's research team, reported some of their findings in an article titled "LifeWay Surveys the Formerly Churched; Can the Church Close the Back Door?" (www.lifewayresearch.com). Waggoner writes that 37 percent of the "formerly churched" said they were "disenchanted with the pastor or church." More specifically, such "disenchantment" was related to the following areas: 17 percent of those surveyed said church members were "hypocritical"; 17 percent said they were "judgmental of others"; 12 percent said the church was "run by a clique that discouraged involvement"; and 14 percent felt the church "was not helping [them] to develop spiritually."

Duin and other researchers have discovered that many disillusioned churchgoers were facing difficult, trying circumstances in their personal lives when they decided to opt out. Some were in desperate need of real help. Their pastors, however, were useless at giving meaningful counsel. The corporate church had let them down. As a result, they were having trouble personally "connecting with God" (p. 22). Duin's research suggests that many churchgoers *are simply not being pastored.* "**Often ministers are out of touch with what's happening on the ground ... [and fail to address] the serious problems many [Christians] face.**" It is no wonder, then, that many people are "no longer content to waste part of their Sundays on an institution that gives them nothing" (p. 23; emphasis added).

Waggoner also notes that **pastors often fail to clearly articulate what God expects of Christians**, causing them to eventually drop out of church. He quotes Greg Ogden's book, *Transforming Discipleship*: "Christian leaders seem to be reluctant to [proclaim] the terms of discipleship that Jesus laid out. What are the reasons for our reluctance? *We are afraid that if we ask too much, people will stop coming to our churches*. Our operating assumption is that people will flee to the nearby 'entertainment church' [those with an emphasis on music, drama and praise-type services] if we ask them to give too much of themselves. So we start with a *low bar* and try to entice people by increments of commitment, hoping that we can raise the bar imperceptibly to the ultimate destination of discipleship" (emphasis added). Waggoner said it appears that some of the formerly churched left because the "destination" was *too slow* emerging.

A similar "out of church" phenomenon is occurring in other countries, such as the UK. According to a 2007 study conducted by the Tearfund organization, only 15 percent of the British population attends church regularly ("Churchgoing in the UK," www.whychurch.org.uk/trends.php). Where are the remaining Brits? Thirty-three percent consider themselves to be non-Christians, and another 33 percent are what the study calls "de-churched"—those who claim to be Christians but choose not to attend church. The study pointed to "poor church experiences" as the main reason so many Brits are de-churched.

Likewise, in New Zealand, historian Andrew Strom notes that would-be churchgoers have been frustrated by a "lack of God." He wrote: "New fads and programs come and go, but mediocrity and *lack of God* just seem to go on forever. And so quietly, sometimes without anyone even noticing, [people] slowly slip out the doors, never to return" (Duin, p. 19). Ultimately, Duin has concluded that Christian leaders as a whole have no idea of the magnitude of the trend of *opting out* of organized religion (p. 19).

The bottom line: **Americans are finding that church is simply no longer *relevant* to their lives**. As Duin says, "what's preached and taught is irrelevant to the questions on the ground" (p. 29). There is a disconnect between what is coming from the pulpit and people's real lives. As one church dropout put it, "One reason churches don't satisfy is that they don't take the gospel seriously.... [They're] not really helping [churchgoers] figure out *how to live* in a way that is glorifying to God in contemporary society" (p. 64).

The church, it seems, has conveniently ignored the raw realities of life. "They're not preaching on real issues—divorce, chastity, cohabitation—that people are facing," says Mike McManus, a syndicated Christian writer. "There's an avoidance of the big issues people are facing.... The church is a big zero when it comes to [educating people on] marriage [issues]" (Duin, pp. 113-114).

For example, Lauren Winner, a former senior editor for *Christianity Today*, has studied the lifestyles of Christian singles (who, as a group, are often neglected by the corporate churches). She found that "**the typical church is clueless about the sexual temptations that flourish**" **in today's society**. "Well-meaning preachers use platitudes, if they say anything at all, to remind their singles to stay celibate." But, more often than not, they *ignore* the thousands of unmarried "Christians" who disobey this injunction (Duin, p. 34). While Winner's outspoken approach has won her few friends in the field of religious journalism, her message is *relevant* to the lives of struggling Christian singles. As Duin notes, sexual issues are especially tough, and church pastors are woefully *negligent* in teaching that it *is* possible to live up to biblical standards of fidelity. They are just not up to dealing with the messiness of life. With such a disconnect from reality, is it any wonder that many single churchgoers "drift off out of shame or frustration" (p. 36)?

In his 2005 book *Revolution*, George Barna writes that a new kind of Christian—he calls them "revolutionaries"—is emerging *out of* the established church. He says these are serious believers—about 20 million strong—who "are not willing to play religious games and aren't interested in being part of a religious community that is not intentionally and aggressively advancing God's Kingdom." Rather, "they are people who want more of God—much more—in their lives. And they are doing whatever it takes to get it"—including *leaving* organized Christianity (p. 7). He adds that today "**millions of devout followers of Jesus Christ are *repudiating tepid systems and practices* of the Christian faith**.... They have no use for churches that play religious games ... [or indulge in] worship services that **drone on without the presence of God** or ministry programs that bear no spiritual fruit." Such revolutionaries, he adds, "eschew ministries that compromise or soft sell our sinful nature" and are "embarrassed by language that promises Christian love and holiness but turns out to be all sizzle and no substance" (pp. 11, 13-14; emphasis added).

CHAPTER TWO

Christian "Worldliness"

While many Americans consider themselves to be Christians, the nation's popular culture, its government and educational institutions, its laws, its entertainment industry, and especially its news media have clearly **become not only un-Christian, but *anti*-Christian**. A veritable tug-of-war has taken place between Christianity and secular culture—and by all accounts, the church isn't winning.

A key reason, according to David Kupelian, is that when the church should have been at the forefront in the country's "culture wars," it too was seduced by worldliness. In his provocative book *The Marketing of Evil*, Kupelian quotes Francis Schaeffer, who is widely regarded as one of the most influential evangelical thinkers and writers of modern times. Schaeffer takes the position that, for the most part, **Christians seem to have drawn back and failed to engage in a meaningful way in the ongoing battle for American culture**. In his book *The Great Evangelical Disaster*, Schaeffer writes: "Most of the evangelical world has not been active in the battle, or even been able to see that we are in a battle" (Kupelian, p. 226). In describing the "failure of the evangelical world to stand for [the] truth," he says **the church has "accommodated" the world—*tried to fit in***. In turn, the "evangelical disaster" has led to the further breakdown of America's culture.

Schaeffer writes that it has been "the weakness and accommodation of the evangelical group on the issues of the day that has been largely responsible for the loss of the Christian ethos" over the past few decades (p. 226). Such accommodation, he writes, is nothing less than "worldliness."

Kupelian suggests that such "accommodation" by evangelical Christians was ostensibly an attempt to gain new converts, the idea being that you have to go where the unconverted are, act like them, look like them—all in hopes of winning their trust. But as we will see, this approach is completely contrary to the biblical instructions. Kupelian gives the following example: "[Youth] pastors at some point started to dispense with their formal attire and instead appeared before teenagers without coat and tie, so as not to appear a stuffed shirt. That's a reasonable accommodation. But what happens when the youth leader's strategy of going tie-less turns into his dressing like a rap singer, talking jive, and wearing earrings? That's what's happening in Christian pop culture today" (p. 228).

Whatever the motive—fear of rejection, doubtfulness, need for acceptance and approval—wanting to fit in and be like the world is just the *opposite* of what Jesus instructed His followers to do. Notice: "I have given them Your words, and the world has hated them because *they are not of the world*, just as I am not of the world" (John 17:14; also verse 16). **The world will despise you if you practice true Christianity because you will be so** *completely different* **in every aspect of your life—because you will refuse to "fit in" and participate in today's popular culture**. James adds: "Pure and undefiled religion before God and the Father is this: to visit orphans and widows in their afflictions, and to *keep oneself unspotted from the world*" (James 1:27).

How many Christians do you know like that?

Perhaps unwittingly, **Christianity has indeed been seduced by those who market popular culture**. In the end, Kupelian argues that we have been seduced because "a hidden, selfish part of us *wanted* to embrace" the falsehoods of secular popular culture (p. 240). Jared Wilson concurs, noting that "in American culture, **it has often become hard to distinguish between the body of Christ and the culture of society**" (*Your Jesus Is Too Safe*, p. 6; emphasis added). Wilson says Christians often quote such passages as "Judge not lest you be judged," or "Let him who is without sin cast the first stone"—because **we want to "justify how we live without the pesky burden of what Jesus requires of us"** (p. 14).

In *Revolution*, Barna laments the considerable "disconnection between what [the Barna Group's] research consistently shows about [the conduct of] churched Christians and what the Bible calls us to [actually] be" (p. 31). If Christians are what they *claim* to be, adds Barna, "their lives should be noticeably and compellingly different from the norm." According to Barna's 2005 data, **of the 77 million Americans who claimed to be churchgoing "born again" Christians, fully *half* of them admitted that they had *not* "experienced a genuine connection" with God over the past year** (p. 32). Moreover, *less than 10 percent* claimed to possess a "biblical worldview"—a core set of beliefs that they have proven as *absolute truth* (the other 90 percent claimed only a patchwork of theological views) (p. 33).

Is it any wonder then that "worldliness" is as much a problem *inside* mainstream Christianity as it is outside?

Youth Opting Out of Church

Disappointed churchgoers are not the only ones saying that church has little to do with the way believers actually *live* their lives. According to David Kinnaman, young *nonbelievers* (which he refers to as "outsiders") are well aware of their peers' "lifestyle gap." In his book *unChristian*, Kinnaman says that "**eighty-five percent of young outsiders have had sufficient exposure to Christians and churches that they conclude present-day Christianity is hypocritical**" (p. 42; emphasis added). He notes that many of these outsiders were once *insiders* who attended church. Now, their negative perception has bled over "into the perspectives of young churchgoers," of which 47 percent *agree* that Christianity has a serious problem with hypocrisy (pp. 42-43).

Thus, young churchgoers are frustrated by what they see—**a failed**

system in which too many Christians simply do not *live* according to their beliefs. As Duin writes, "when church isn't *relevant*, the first ones out the door are usually the young" (p. 37). She points to mid-2006 research which suggests that, at current dropout rates, *only four percent* of American teens will end up as Bible-believing churchgoers (compare this to 35 percent of baby boomers and 65 percent of their World War II-era grandparents).

Drew Dyck, a lead researcher for *Christianity Today*, writes on the magazine's Web site that the May 2009 Pew Forum on Religion and Public Life reports that "young Americans are dropping out of religion at an alarming rate of *five to six times* the historic rate" ("The 'Leavers': Young Doubters Exit the Church"; www.christianitytoday.com/ct/2010/november/27.40.html?start=1).

Dyck also notes that, according to Rainer Research, approximately 70 percent of America's young people drop out of church between the ages of 18 and 22. Similarly, the Barna Group estimates that 80 percent of those reared in the church will be "disengaged" by the time they are 29.

The epidemic of young people leaving the established church does not mean they have given up on God, just the failed system. Young people do not resonate with what is being presented to them in church. Christian author Steve Mansfield says young people "are voting with their feet. **The next generation is not going to church**. For the most part, they are going to the First Church of Starbucks"—where they will sit, drinking a latte and studying *relevant* Christian teaching material. This, Mansfield says, is the *future of the church*. "In fifteen years, present trends continuing, the church in America will be half of what it [now] is" (Duin, p. 38; emphasis added).

Duin writes that many frustrated Christians, especially those of the younger generation, are "creating their own wineskins instead of dealing with the current structure" (p. 33). The failure of the one-size-fits-all corporate church has forced them into the *parachurch* sector—home fellowships, small-group meetings, coffeehouse studies, reliance on printed materials or Internet ministries. They understand that the church is the *spiritual* body of Christ (I Cor. 12:13), and cannot be defined by corporate charters or contained by bricks and mortar.

Young Adults Walking Away from Christianity

While many in their 20s and 30s are opting out of organized religion, a significant number are actually walking away from *Christianity itself*. Dyck has studied this phenomenon and sees a significant trend developing among young adults. In his Web article noted above, he writes that **"sociologists are seeing a major shift taking place *away from* Christianity" among young Americans**.

Referencing the results of the 2009 American Religious Identification Survey (ARIS), Dyck notes that the percentage of Americans claiming "no religious affiliation" has almost doubled in about two decades—from 8.1 percent in 1990 to 15 percent in 2008. The trend has been fairly uniform across the nation—even in the so-called Bible belt. Significantly, 22 percent of 18- to 29-year-olds claimed to be "unaffiliated"—up from 11 percent in 1990. Moreover, 73 percent of those came from "religious" homes, and **an amazing 66 percent described themselves as "de-converts"—meaning they had** *opted out* **of Christianity altogether.**

Based on his thousands of interviews with young adults, Kinnaman likewise concludes: "The vast majority of outsiders [those who do not claim to be Christian] in this country, particularly among young generations, are actually *de-churched* individuals" (*unChristian*, p. 74). As the *de-churched*, he refers to Dyck's "de-converts"—those who were once part of the Christian community, but no longer consider themselves to be Christian. Again, they're not just church dropouts, disenchanted with corporate religion; they have, in Kinnaman's terms, put Christianity itself "on the shelf" (p. 74). In other words, **the problem of today's young adults leaving the church is not just about their becoming** *un*-**Christian, it's also about them choosing to become** *ex*-**Christians**.

But why are so many young people turning their backs on Christianity? According to Dyck, the answer is complex. He notes that there is a subgroup of young Christians who have chosen to drop out of church because of abuse—those he calls *recoilers*. In an interview with *The Christian Post*, Dyck said recoilers are those who have left the faith because of "painful childhood or teenage experiences with the church." He adds: "They have become disillusioned with faith because the people they sanctified let them down. God is guilty by association" (Michelle Vul, *The Christian Post*, Jan. 6, 2011; Vul discusses Dyck's new book, *Generation Ex-Christian*; www.christianpost.com/article/20110106/generation-ex-christian-uncovers-why-people-leave-the-faith/).

However, Dyck points largely to one key factor: *moral compromise*. Many young Christians, he writes, experience an unbearable level of "conflict between belief and behavior. Tired of dealing with a guilty conscience and **unwilling to abandon their sinful lifestyles, they drop their Christian commitment**. They may cite intellectual skepticism or disappointments with the church, but these are smokescreens designed to hide the [real] reason. [In effect,] **they change their creed to match their deeds**…" (emphasis added).

While some young people have had distinct "postmodern misgivings"—that is, they have fundamental difficulties with the teachings of mainstream Christianity—or may have experienced some form of abuse associated with church, most young adults who abandon the faith do so in order to **adopt a lifestyle that falls outside the bounds of Christian morality**. **Ultimately, they desire worldliness instead of godliness.**

As Dyck rightly notes, "the Christian life is hard to sustain in the face of so many temptations"—especially for the younger generation. But Dyck has come to the conclusion that it is the church itself that has *failed* to equip young people to fight the good fight. "I realized that **most 'leavers'** had been exposed to [only] a superficial form of Christianity that effectively inoculated them against authentic faith" (emphasis added). Kinnaman has come to a similar conclusion: "It is easy to embrace a *costless* form of Christianity in America today, and we [the church leadership] have probably contributed to that by **giving [young] people a superficial understanding of the gospel** and focusing only on their decision to convert" (p. 75; emphasis added).

"Churchanity's" narrow-minded rush to increase membership rolls has led to the development of spiritually weak, ill-prepared converts—particularly among young people. Instead of emphasizing personal transformation and practical faith according to Scripture, young people have been sold a *feel-good religion*—one that fails miserably when stacked up against the pulls and temptations of society.

According to Dyck, when sociologists examined the spiritual lives of American teenagers, they found that most teens were practicing a religion best described as "Moralistic Therapeutic Deism"—which "casts God as a distant Creator who blesses people who are good, nice and fair." The central goal in such a religion is to help believers "be happy and feel good" about themselves. Where did teenagers learn this "faith"? Unfortunately, says Dyck, it's one "taught, implicitly and sometimes explicitly, at every age level in many churches. It's in the air that many churchgoers breathe, from seeker-friendly worship services to low-commitment small groups. When this naive and coldly utilitarian view of God crashes on the hard rocks of reality"—the trials and temptations of real life—"we shouldn't be surprised to see people of any age walk away" from Christianity.

Barna Group research shows that *only three percent* of young people who say they have (or had) made a commitment to follow Christ possess a clearly-defined set of beliefs based on the Scriptures, particularly in the area of absolute *moral* truth. As Kinnaman notes, "What Scripture teaches is the primary grid for [young people] making decisions and interacting with the world" (p. 75). When that "grid" is not in place—when all you have is a "feel-good" religion—morality is the first thing out the window. Ultimately, in a "lightweight [emotionally-based] exposure to Christianity, where a decision for Christ is portrayed as simple and costless, [the experience] will fail to produce lasting faith in young people" (Kinnaman, p. 76).

Compounding the problem is the fact that many young people who express their concerns or doubts about Christianity are often ridiculed or treated with contempt. Dyck writes that in his interviews with young people who have left the faith, numerous de-converts reported "sharing their burgeoning doubts with a Christian friend or family member only to receive trite, unhelpful answers."

This utter failure to engage young believers in a relevant, Bible-based, life-changing faith experience falls squarely at the feet of America's ministers and pastors. **But too many "Christian" leaders do not really believe or follow the Bible themselves—so how can they be expected to**

teach our young people to do so? Today's so-called Christianity is based largely on carefully selected New Testament passages (mostly from Paul's writings) that are twisted to make them appear to teach a "soft Christianity"—a *costless* "faith" void of works and indifferent to clear biblical teachings. Thus, the typical teenager's "conversion" is based on a fleeting emotional experience wherein the new "believer" is enamored with a popularized, bumper-sticker "Jesus." But without an *informed* biblical foundation centered on personal change, works and obedience—with a corresponding network of support from mature Christians—the young person will soon discover that their "religion" is of little help when it comes to facing the pressures of this world.

CHAPTER THREE

New Age Religion—Filling the Gap

While many young people are opting out of organized religion, a sizable minority of "leavers" have adopted *alternative* spiritualities. Religion writer Jon Meacham wrote a piece in the April 13, 2009, edition of *Newsweek* titled "The End of Christian America." According to Meacham, Christians are now making up a *steadily declining* percentage of the American population. Referencing 2009 ARIS results, he writes that the percentage of Americans who identify themselves as Christians has fallen ten percentage points since 1990, from 86 to 76 percent. Apparently, **Americans are becoming increasingly non-religious or they are turning to alternate religions—such as Eastern forms of spirituality or other "New Age" religions**.

During this same time period, according to ARIS figures, the number of people willing to describe themselves as atheists or agnostic has increased from 1 million to 3.6 million. This strongly indicates movement toward non-Christian religions, as many of those who are now describing themselves as "agnostic" are actually anti-Christianity. In other words, **Americans who were previously "religiously unaffiliated"—including those who have become entirely disenchanted with Christianity—are increasingly turning to New Age and Eastern religions as alternatives to Christianity**.

Meacham writes that "many conservative Christians believe [America] has now entered a post-Christian phase." (In this context, post-Christian describes a significant *decline* in the importance of Christianity in society.) Albert Mohler, president of the Southern Baptist Theological Seminary, one of the largest in the world, shares this viewpoint: "The post-Christian narrative ... offers spirituality, however defined, *without binding authority* [that is, a form of "spirituality" *lacking* clearly-established authority, such as provided by the Scriptures]. It is based on [a perspective] of history that presumes a less tolerant past [such as under rigid, conservative evangelicalism] and [the expectation of] a more tolerant future [such as found in New Age-type religions where virtually anything goes and all viewpoints have validity], with the present as an important transitional step." Meacham adds that **what we see happening in Christianity today "is less about the death of [the Christian] God and more about the *birth of many gods*"—New Age pantheism.**

As mainstream Christianity fails to deliver on its promises, more and more churchgoers are reaffirming their faith through small, home-based fellowship groups. Others, however, are reaching the unfortunate conclusion that God (as they define Him) is not limited to Christianity—that He can be found through other forms of "spirituality." This, at least in part, explains the recent upsurge in New Age forms of religion.

New Age "spirituality" is a catch-all for various *blends* of Eastern-styled "faiths" such as Hinduism, Buddhism, etc.—including several off-beat occult type religions. New Age religion revolves around one central theme (with minor variations). In his book *Understanding the New Age*, Russell Chandler says this theme can be summed up in three words: *All is one.* He explains that in New Age mysticism humans have a suppressed or hidden "higher self" that reflects the divine element of the universe. This "higher self" *is* the New Age God, sometimes referred to as "Infinite Intelligence" or "Ultimate Reality." Chandler gives the following formula: "All is One. We are all One. All is God. And we are God" (p. 29). **This pantheistic theme teaches that God is *in* everything and *in* everyone—thus, *you are God.***

According to New Age teachings, everything one needs for a life of contentment, purpose and fulfillment comes from *inside* of you—love, peace, joy, the *truth.* All such "divine qualities" are universal and are innately part of your innermost being—your "essence identity." You only have to "quiet the mind"—which mostly tends to hinder your quest for "enlightenment"—and "tune in" as it were to your true, inner self. Evil does not exist; the undesirable aspects of your existence (your dysfunctional, selfish, materialistic nature) are not really you; they are part of the *mind*, from which you must free yourself.

Contrast this with what Jesus taught, that **the human heart is actually a source of deceit, evil, pride and corruption** (Mark 7:15-23). The prophet Jeremiah wrote that **the human heart is deceitful and "desperately wicked"** (Jer. 17:9). Indeed, there is a way that *seems right* to the human mind, but it only leads to death (Prov. 14:12).

One of the leading forces in New Age religion worldwide is Eckhart Tolle, with two "spirituality" best-sellers: *The Power of Now* and *A New Earth—Awakening to Your Life's Purpose.* Tolle writes: "I cannot tell you any spiritual truth that deep within you don't already know.... Living knowledge, ancient and yet ever new, is there [inside you] ... [waiting to be] activated and released from within every cell of your body" (*The Power of Now*, p. 9).

In New Age mysticism, truth is never defined, it just *is.* "The Truth is inseparable from who you are. Yes, you *are* the Truth. If you look for it elsewhere, you will be deceived every time. The very Being that you are is Truth" (*A New Earth*, p. 71). Moreover, **commandment-keeping—a fundamental part of the Christian way of life—is deemed irrelevant in New Age philosophy.** "When you are in touch with that [divine] dimension ... all your actions and relationships will reflect the oneness with all life that you sense deep within. This is love. Laws, commandments, rules, and regulations are necessary [only] for those who are cut off from who they are, the Truth within" (p. 72).

Such perverted religious psycho-babble can potentially influence unsuspecting Christians—especially those who are tempted to look outside of Christianity for spiritual fulfillment. Chandler writes that while New Age motifs are being "openly embraced" by the more liberal elements of Christianity, New Age groups "often co-opt the language and trappings of the traditional Christian churches, thereby making newcomers feel more comfortable in their transition to alternate forms of belief and practice" (p. 207). The highly popular media mogul Oprah Winfrey, a huge supporter of New Age spirituality, sponsors a "mind training" program called "A Course in Miracles." According to Chandler, the much-touted course—which espouses a worldview in which there is no sin, no evil, no devil, and where God is *in* everyone and everything—is "couched in Christian terminology with a psychological application" (p. 212). **Why would a New Age "spirituality" course need to use Christian terminology—except to seduce naive Christians?**

Another key New Age proponent, Deepak Chopra, has recently turned his sights on Christianity with his menacing book, *The Third Jesus*. Chopra, a self-styled "spiritual" writer and Eastern guru, has been a major force behind the rapid growth of New Age spiritualism in America over the past four decades. According to his book, Jesus' teachings on morality and conduct were "too radical to live by" (p. 2). Stressing what he calls the impractical nature of Jesus' instructions, he writes: "You can struggle your entire life to be a good Christian without succeeding in doing what Jesus explicitly wanted." But what Chopra and others like him fail to understand is that, with God, *all things are possible* (Matt. 19:26). While God does not expect Christians to become perfect in *this* life, we are to be working diligently *towards* perfection—to be conformed (a process) to the image of Christ (Rom. 8:29). Ultimately, such conversion and transformation is impossible without the Holy Spirit of God.

Rather than taking Jesus' teachings literally—do unto others as you would have them do unto you (Matt. 7:12); love your enemies, bless those who curse you (Matt. 5:44); resist not evil, but turn the other cheek (Matt. 5:39); etc.—Chopra claims that Jesus was actually pointing His disciples "toward a mystical realm, the only place where human nature can radically change" (p. 2). Literal obedience to practical laws and commandments is replaced by the "radical and mystical" path of seeking "God consciousness" (p. 10). Shockingly, he writes that "Christianity was forced to *compromise* Jesus' vision…. It's easy to see why the new world Christ envisioned was so quickly abandoned after He died. It had to be modified by realists" (pp. 3, 18). Accordingly, Jesus' plan could only be accomplished by attaining the "highest level of enlightenment." "Our task," he writes, "is to delve into Scripture and prove that a map to enlightenment exists there" (p. 10).

Disastrously, Chopra's unbiblical "worldview" has found significant favor among "Christians" who despise commandment-keeping. After all, we are by nature antagonistic towards God's laws and precepts (Rom 8:7). Only God knows how many weak, fence-riding Christians have fallen for such demon-inspired psycho-babble. Indeed, **a key reason for the appeal of New Age religions is that they, like "cost-less Christianity," require little or nothing in the way of commitment or fidelity to a standard of conduct**. New Age practitioners essentially live as they please; moral absolutes simply don't exist. Their much-sought-after "state of enlightenment" essentially puts them on the *same level as God*. Adam and Eve tried this—"you shall be as gods, *deciding good and evil*"—and look where it has brought us.

Devout Christians who study their Bibles can readily see the dangers in New Age teachings. Ultimately, New Age religion is a feel-good invent-your-own form of "spirituality" that can lead to contact with "the prince of the power of the air [Satan the devil], the spirit that is now working within the children of disobedience" (Eph. 2:2). Unfortunately, **too many young people are opting for such "religions" because they are turned off by a "Christianity" that apparently makes no real difference in their lives**. As mainstream Christianity continues to decline for numerous reasons—not the least of which is its *utter ineffectiveness*—more and more Americans (especially the younger ones) will be tempted to experiment with various New Age/Eastern religions. Most, however, will seek out a brand of Christianity they can call their own—but it will definitely be *outside* of the "brick and mortar" corporate church.

Finding God—*Outside* of the Corporate Church

As previously noted, 2009 ARIS statistics show that the number of Americans who claim *no religious affiliation* has nearly doubled since 1990, rising from 8.1 to 15 percent. According to Meacham, "The rising numbers of religiously unaffiliated Americans are people more apt to call themselves *spiritual* rather than *religious*." Other studies have indicated that about 40 percent of this "unaffiliated" group turn out to be atheists. The remaining 60 percent—still a significant number of Americans—claim to be merely "religious" or "spiritual" without identifying a particular religious preference.

As we've seen, some of these have turned to various New Age religions. But Duin suggests that these and related statistics show that **there are plenty of Americans who are interested in spiritual matters, but prefer to find spiritual fulfillment outside of *organized* Christianity** (p. 13). To put it another way, more and more Americans are apparently claiming to be "unaffiliated" because of their disenchantment with organized Christianity. They still consider themselves to be Christian, but are intent on finding God in an alternate setting—such as small groups and home-based fellowships.

Duin writes of numerous trendsetters who are forging ahead with strategies to meet the needs of those believers who prefer to remain *outside* of the established church. One such evangelical leader, Mark Batterson, began in 1996 to promote "coffeehouse churches" in the Washington, DC area. In an interview with Duin, he said, "God is calling the church out of the church. We love the marketplace [coffeehouse] environment because the de-churched and unchurched people are intimidated by [traditional] church" (p. 74).

Another trendsetter, Louis Brown, says 80 percent of the American population claims to be "faith-based," but only 18 percent go to church. Brown, co-producer of *The Bible Experience*, an audio dramatization of the Bible aimed at young people, asks, "So *where* are they getting their faith content?" (p. 44).

For the unchurched who truly *are* "faith-based," they are finding it at *home*. According to a 2006 Barna Group survey, **nine percent of American adults are involved in some form of house church** (this equates to 20 million people attending such a "service" each week). The balance of unchurched believers attend similar small-group meetings; some bounce back and forth—mostly going to church on Sunday and participating in a midweek home study. Still, the "church at home" trend is clearly gaining momentum.

Shane Claiborne—author of the controversial book *The Irresistible Revolution*, in which Claiborne describes what he considers an authentic faith rooted in action—is solidly behind the idea that "smaller is better." In an interview with Duin, he said, **"The world is thirsty for another way of life. Our culture is starving for answers, as the old ones have gone bankrupt"** (p. 44; emphasis added). Small groups and home fellowships, he said, are "giving visibility to Christianity as a *way of living* rather than as just a way of believing.... [There is] more to Christianity than just believing. When people see there are ways of living that don't conform to the patterns of the world, that is very attractive" (p. 43). Here, Claiborne suggests what has been verified by Kinnaman in his book *unChristian*—that nominal Christianity is seen by outsiders as more of a "set of beliefs" than a genuine *way of life*.

Barna fully supports the idea of church at home. Of his own experience, he says, "It's the best thing we've ever done.... Everyone in the [home] church is really involved. We really look out for each other. It is one big extended family of twenty-three people" (Duin, p. 59).

According to researchers, many of those who are moving on to home churches say they are tired of church hierarchies that are too controlling. They are also fed up with church politics. But, as Duin notes, those who do not fit into standard "churchanity" also realize that they *need* like-minded fellowship—that they cannot simply opt out of the body of Christ. They have come to see that the true church is *spiritual*—where "two or three people get together" in Jesus' name (p. 61; see Matt. 18:20). Attendance is based on desire rather than obligation.

A 2007 Barna Group study demonstrated that Christians had a "higher level of satisfaction" with their house church than they did with regular church. Barna concludes that those attracted to house churches are either *young adults* interested in finding spirituality and faith—but who are turned off by the organized church—or *baby boomers* who are seeking a deeper and more intense experience with God (Duin, p. 61).

CHAPTER FOUR

From Pablum to Heresy

Research clearly shows that a huge factor in churchgoers deciding to leave church is *mediocre* teaching. Concerning this lack of relevant content from the pulpit, Duin says time-strapped pastors often download sermon material off the Internet. A tremendous number of pastors get their material off of Rick Warren's Saddleback Church site (www.pastors.com) and Joel Osteen's resources site (www.joelosteen.com). According to those who have studied this issue—such as Haddon Robinson of Gordon-Conwell Theological Seminary—online "borrowing" is "a national problem. If [pastors] do this regularly, [their] brain shrivels up" (p. 103). Patrick Reardon, theology professor at Ambridge, Pennsylvania, suggests the problem is much worse—that pastors are "intellectually lazy. **The average evangelical pastor is not a man of the Scriptures. In fact, they are very weak on the Scriptures**…" (Duin, p. 104; emphasis added). Reardon faults today's churches for their overall lack of substance, noting that they appear to be more interested in novel programs and marketing schemes designed to attract new members. Meanwhile, the members they already have "are seriously famished. They have not had a serious [spiritual] meal in years."

Research conducted in 2006 by LifeWay again pointed to a rapid decline in church attendance. For example, the number of Americans who identified themselves as Southern Baptists dropped from 10 percent in 1995 to just six percent in 2001. LifeWay's Brad Waggoner wanted to know why. He found that many **churches have done a poor job of grounding people in their faith and explaining what it really means to make a commitment to be Christian**. According to Waggoner, the typical church is not educating people by teaching Scripture in an understandable and applicable way (Duin, p. 108). Writing in a 2006 column in *Christianity Today*, Chuck Colson reported that what is now being offered in church "is just getting dumbed down more and more." He points to an overemphasis on worship music. "Music is important in the life of the church…. But it cannot take the place of solid teaching" (p. 108).

Other experts told Duin that churchgoers "are sick, mentally ill, furious, and angry with life. If the church wants to meet people's needs, it needs to find a way of teaching people so they really [know how to] change their lives" (p. 106). Detroit Anglican priest Richard Kim told Duin that "**the church [has become] irrelevant, boring and powerless. The gospel is not preached; or, where it is preached, it is usually in philosophical blah-blah language void of the power of God**" (p. 109; emphasis added). The well-known New York-based evangelist David Wilkerson said, "The messages being brought forth from pulpits are comprised of motivational pep talks, jokes and entertainment. It's all spiritual baby food…." He says *repentance is not being taught* in the churches, and wonders if pastors are afraid of offending their flocks and losing numbers (p. 110).

This is reminiscent of the prophet Isaiah's warning concerning those "who say to the seers, 'See not,' [don't tell us about God's coming judgment] and to the prophets [teachers], '**Do not prophesy to us right things [such as repentance from sin], speak to us smooth things, prophesy illusions**' " (Isa. 30:10). Tell us things to make us feel good about ourselves; tell us God is pleased with us as Christians. But there is perhaps no greater *illusion* than to think that one "has it all together" as a Christian. In His corrective letter to the church of the Laodiceans, Jesus warned of this very attitude—of being self-satisfied, complacent, having "need of nothing" (Rev. 3:14-21).

In his 2007 book *Loving God When You Don't Love the Church*, pastor Chris Jackson says he is running into a lot of people who are disillusioned. Their Christian experience is not the life-changing experience they thought it would be. "**The hunger in people today is for a combination of** *practical truth they can apply and experience*. People are looking for Jesus, period. If they found a place they felt embodied a relationship with Him, far fewer people would leave the church" (Duin, p. 116; emphasis added). One disappointed dropout told Duin, "There is little or no teaching on how to *die to ourselves* [repentance] and what that might look like. Nor are we taught how to live by faith and what that looks like…. *We are missing the power of the Holy Spirit…*" (p. 112; emphasis added). Duin concludes that there is "much more to the Christian life than we are experiencing, but we do not know [are not being taught] how to find it or what it looks like."

According to research by the Barna Group, there is a "huge gap between the perception of pastors and the reality of the people's devotion to God. Pastors evaluate spiritual health from an institutional perspective—that is, are people involved in keeping the system going—while [only] people [themselves] are aware of their unmet need to have a deeper and more meaningful relationship with God" (Duin, p. 128). Churchgoers need to hear preaching on child rearing, marriage, divorce, chastity, godliness, unanswered prayer—the real issues people are facing. But there seems to be an avoidance of such key issues. Why? Are pastors simply incompetent, out of touch, in over their heads—or are they afraid of offending their congregations?

Compounding this "pablum for substance" problem is the fact that churchgoers are not being taught how to *study* their Bibles. A survey conducted by the Willow Creek Church of South Barrington, Illinois, led researchers to the conclusion that **much of Christianity has failed to teach believers how to become "self-feeders"—how to read and study their Bibles on their own** (Duin, p. 172).

On the flip side of all this are those who are *quite satisfied* with the pablum coming from today's pulpits. For them, church is nothing more than a social club. They have embraced what Duin calls a "costless Christianity that's easily maintained" (p. 116). Jesus corrected the religious hobbyists of His day for this very same approach: "*Hypocrites!* Isaiah has prophesied well concerning you, saying, '**These people have drawn near to Me [God] with their mouths, and with their lips they honor Me**' "—**they say all the right things, sing praises to God every Sunday morning, etc.—**" '**but their hearts are far away from Me**. For they **worship Me in vain**, teaching for doctrine the commandments of men' " (Matt. 15:7-9). They teach *what men want to hear*— "smooth things."

Likewise, the prophet Jeremiah wrote: "An astounding and horrible thing has happened in the land. The prophets [pastors] prophesy [teach] falsely, and the priests bear rule by their means; and *My people love to have it so...*" (Jer. 5:30-31). They love to hear "soft doctrine"—but nothing that will prick their consciences. **And their "pastors" willingly oblige—they preach only what the people want to hear**, **for fear of offending their congregations and losing their income or lofty positions**.

Ezekiel also wrote of such "churchgoers": "[The] children of your people are ... speaking to one another, each man to his brother, saying, 'I pray you, **come and hear what is the word [preached]** which comes forth from the LORD.' And they come to you [pastors] as the people [have traditionally] come, and **they sit before you as My people** [on Sunday mornings], and *they hear your words*. **But they will not do them**." *Why?* They have not been taught *true repentance* of sin or to reverence God's commandments. "**For with their mouth *they show much love* [again, they *say* all the right things; they *sound like* Christians], but their heart goes after their covetousness**" (Ezek. 33:30-31). Such "love" is only a counterfeit, as opposed to the genuine *love of God* instilled by the Holy Spirit into the lives of true believers (Rom. 5:5).

They "talk the talk," but do not "walk the walk." They love to *look* and *sound* like good Christians, but they do not want to do the *works* of a real Christian—do not want to give up their way of life: adultery, fornication, divorce, alcohol abuse, materialism, etc. **They have bought into the lie of "costless Christianity"—a "Christianity" void of godly works, void of overcoming the pulls and weaknesses of the flesh; a religion in name only, in which adherents profess the name of Christ, but *practice sin* as a way of life**.

In ignorance, many nominal Christians are practicing a form of "grace turned to license." In II Thessalonians two, the apostle Paul warned of what he called the "mystery of lawlessness" (verse 7)—the very spirit or mindset behind "costless Christianity." Paul wrote that this "mystery" was *already at work* in his time as nominal Christians were embracing "grace" without corresponding good works or obedience to the commandments of God.

Like the *Laodiceans* of the apostle John's day, such churchgoers are *blind* to their true spiritual condition. To them Jesus says: "I know your works, that you are neither cold nor hot; I would that you be either cold or hot. So then, because you are lukewarm, and are neither cold nor hot, I will spew you out of My mouth. For you say, 'I am [spiritually] rich, and have become wealthy, and have need of nothing'; and you do not understand that you are wretched, and miserable, and poor, and blind, and naked.

"I counsel you to buy from Me gold purified by fire so that you may be rich; and white garments [righteousness—obedience to God's laws] so that you may be clothed, and the shame of your nakedness may not be revealed; and to anoint your eyes with eye salve, so that you may see. As many as I love, I rebuke and chasten. Therefore, **be zealous and repent**. Behold, I stand at the door and knock. If anyone hears My voice and opens the door, I will come in to him, and will sup with him, and he with Me" (Rev. 3:15-20). Notice that no true relationship exists between God and such nominal Christians; God is in fact on the *outside*—at the door, urging repentance.

Indeed, Satan—a true master of seduction—is skillfully and subtly using powerful spiritual weapons to render the church impotent. As we have seen, incompetence, ignorance and negligence on the part of too many pastors have been key factors in the overall failure of American "churchanity." And while church pastors typically have the best of intentions, many are, by biblical standards, nothing more than *false ministers*.

CHAPTER FIVE

False Teachers Work from *Within* Churches

The Bible reveals that not all who claim to "preach the Word" are *true* ministers of Christ. There are numerous references in Scripture to *false prophets*. In Old Testament times, a false prophet was one who claimed divine inspiration, but actually made *false* proclamations (I Kings 22:10-14, 17).

The New Testament warns that there will be false prophets *working deceit* and *teaching falsehoods* until Jesus' return. However, the Greek term used for prophet in the New Testament is rarely used of those who attempt to foretell the future. Rather, in the early church, "prophet" had a broader meaning, referring primarily to those who preach the Word of God as pastors, ministers or evangelists—those who "proclaim the divine message with special preparation and with a special mission" (Arndt and Gingrich, *A Greek-English Lexicon of the New Testament*). Still, the use of "prophet" in many Old Testament passages (such as Jeremiah 5:31, etc.) can have a parallel application, referring to today's Christian "pastor."

Thus, when Jesus warned, "beware of false prophets who come to you in sheep's clothing, for within they are [actually] ravening wolves," He was referring to *pastors* and *teachers* who—with deliberate deceit or in ignorance—would bring *false* teachings into churches. Jesus went on to say, "You shall know them by their fruits…" (Matt. 7:15-16). Thus, you are to be examining *any* teacher or pastor who presumes to preach the Bible—to discern their fruits.

Jesus Himself is the only perfect Pastor and Shepherd. All others must be tested. Jesus said of Himself, "I am the door. If anyone enters through Me, he shall be saved, and shall go in and out, and shall find pasture. The thief [false teacher or pastor] does not come except to steal and kill and destroy. I have come so that [you] may have life, and may have it more abundantly" (John 10:9-10). In the final days before His crucifixion, Jesus also warned against false teachers who would preach deceiving messages. **"Be on guard, so that no one deceives you. For many shall come in My name, saying, 'I [Jesus] am [indeed] the Christ'; and [yet] they shall deceive many"** (Matt. 24:4-5).

This passage is truly amazing. Many, *not just a few*, but *many* preachers and pastors will come *in Jesus' name*—in apparent full support of the Christian religion—teaching that *Jesus* is indeed the Christ. (This verse cannot refer to those messianic impostors who would come claiming that *they* themselves are the Christ, for it is impossible to come *in the name of Jesus* and simultaneously claim to *be* the Christ.) How is it that preachers and pastors can teach Jesus as the Christ—and yet deceive many? By teaching a "costless" *carnal-friendly*

Christianity—one that professes the name of Christ but denies the way of life of genuine obedience necessary for salvation (Rom. 2:13).

Notice this key passage Jesus gave concerning those who would unknowingly serve Him in vain:

> "Not everyone who says to Me [or calls Me], 'Lord, Lord,' shall enter into the kingdom of heaven; **but the one who is doing the will of My Father**, Who is in heaven. Many [again, not the few] will say to Me in that day, 'Lord, Lord, did we not prophesy [preach] through Your name? And did we not cast out demons through Your name? And did we not perform many works of power through Your name?' And then I will confess to them, 'I never knew you. Depart from Me, **you who work lawlessness**.' [They talked the talk, but did not walk the walk.] Therefore, everyone who **hears these words of Mine and practices them**, I will compare him to a wise man, who built his house upon the rock; and the rain came down, and the floods came, and the winds blew, and beat upon that house; but it did not fall, for it was founded upon the rock. And everyone **who hears these words of Mine and does not practice them** shall be compared to a foolish man, who built his house upon the sand; and the rain came down, and the floods came, and the winds blew, and beat upon that house; and it fell, and great was the fall of it" (Matt. 7:21-27).

Is it possible that the overwhelming majority of today's Christian leaders and pastors have carelessly produced a weak, watered-down "costless Christianity"—which has *pacified* the typical "social Christian" but *neglected* the spiritual needs of serious churchgoers? Moreover, is it possible that *some* ministers and pastors are being *used* by Satan to subvert Christianity?

Satan is *actively deceiving* the entire world (Rev. 12:9). Christians today need to be aware of the subtle methods Satan uses to carry out his insidious plans. We need to be on guard against his crafty devices, "so that we may not be outwitted by Satan, for we are not [to be] ignorant of his schemes" (II Cor. 2:11). In the first century AD, while most of the original apostles were still alive and ministering to the churches, false teachers worked their way into local congregations. They subtly took control, often casting out true ministers. Yet they did so *thinking* they were serving God. Never underestimate the power of Satan—for he is quite able to *use* people for his diabolical purposes.

According to Paul, **Satan has his *own* ministers who *appear* as ministers of righteousness** (II Cor. 11:15) . They are not genuinely following Christ, but they *think* they are; they are not teaching the Bible in a meaningful, life-changing manner, but they *think* they are. How many "Christian" pastors are, unknowingly, ministers of Satan? How many of such

23

"ministers" sit on doctrinal boards or have teaching positions in church colleges? How much control have they taken to themselves over what you believe and practice? How much of God's truth have they changed, watered-down, liberalized or just plain ignored?

Blind Leaders of the Blind

Writing to the church in Corinth, the apostle Paul gives a stern warning concerning those who had *handled the Word of God deceitfully* (II Cor. 4:2). To accomplish his sinister purpose, Satan stirs up false teachers and false ministers to *mislead* believers with false doctrines. Perhaps *unknowingly*, they do so through the *misuse* of Scripture. Again, they too are deceived—they simply do not realize they are teaching error.

But because they quote the Bible and say all the "right" things, people gullibly accept it as truth. Their misguided interpretations of God's Word are often backed by clever theological arguments with intellectual-sounding words. On the surface, their teachings *appear* to be words of wisdom, logic and truth—but they are not "rightly dividing the Word of the truth" (II Tim. 2:15). Yes, they use Scripture, but they *divide* it wrongly.

The result is that they and their followers are *blinded* to the truth of God. **When believers willingly follow pastors and teachers who have *blinded themselves* to the truth of God, they too become blind**. Jesus warned His followers to "be on guard against the *leaven* of the Pharisees and Sadducees," meaning their teachings (Matt. 16:6-12). These Jewish leaders taught that their human traditions were greater than the commandments of God. Jesus denounced them, saying they had "made void the commandment [truth] of God for the sake of [their] tradition" (Matt. 15:6). As quoted earlier, He went on to say that they had worshipped God *in vain*, putting tradition above Scripture (verses 7-9).

How much of what you believe and practice is based on *tradition*? How much of what you believe and practice is based on the unadulterated Word of God? Are you unknowingly following "blind leaders of the blind" (Matt. 15:14)?

Paul warned the Corinthians that they were being drawn away from the true gospel by **self-serving "pastors" who were handling the Word of God improperly**. The Corinthian believers were accepting false teachings from false teachers—and beginning to lose what Paul had already taught them. In his second epistle to the Corinthians, Paul warned them concerning their spiritual folly: "But I fear, lest by any means, as the serpent deceived Eve by his craftiness [subtle, true-sounding lies], **so your minds might be corrupted from the simplicity that is in Christ**. For indeed, if someone comes preaching *another* Jesus, whom we did not preach, or you receive a *different* spirit, which you did not [originally] receive, or a *different* gospel, which you did not [originally] accept, **you put up with it as something good**" (II Cor. 11:3-4).

The apostle Peter warned of false pastors and ministers who would bring heretical teachings into the church. "But there were also false prophets among the people [in Old Testament times], as indeed **there will be false teachers among you** [within your congregations], **who will stealthily introduce destructive heresies** [we will list some of these in a later chapter], personally denying the Lord who bought them, and bringing swift destruction upon themselves. And **many people will follow as authoritative their destructive ways**; and because of them, the way of the truth will be blasphemed" (II Pet. 2:1-2).

Could this be happening in *your* church? Don't be too sure it isn't! Remember, Satan has *his* ministers who *say* all the "right-sounding" things (II Cor. 11:15). What comes from many pulpits *sounds* convincing and *appears* to be backed by Scripture. But is it really?

What *is* the spiritual condition of your church? How does your pastor *handle* the Word of God? What are the doctrinal teachings of your church? Are you being taught doctrines which *sound* true, but are contrary to the Bible? Could you be blinded and deceived into actually denying the truth of God?

Jude's Powerful Warning

Jude, the brother of Jesus, wrote his urgent epistle to believers because they were in danger of being ensnared by deception—from *within* the church. He wrote: "For certain men have *stealthily crept in*, those who long ago have been written about, condemning them to this judgment. They are ungodly men, who are **perverting the grace of our God, turning it into licentiousness**, and are personally denying the only Lord God and our Lord Jesus Christ" (Jude 4).

The popular Protestant teaching that Jesus somehow abolished the Law or "kept it in our stead" is at the heart of "costless Christianity"—grace turned to license. Scripture is clear that salvation *is* by grace alone, that works cannot *earn* one justification with God. But in no way does grace remove the requirement that the believer *live a life of obedience* to God's laws and commandments. Carnal-friendly "Christianity" denies Jesus of His position as Lord and Master of our lives—it robs the Word of God of its life-changing power.

The words of Paul and Jude have been preserved as warnings for us today. Paul declared that in the *last days* there would be men—pastors, teachers and preachers—who would *appear* to be godly, but who would deny the power of God by their *failure* to teach obedience to *all* of God's commandments and their failure to emphasize good works (II Tim. 3:1, 5).

Duin writes that, for some, there is "more spiritual danger in staying in church than going it alone" (*Quitting Church*, p. 112). Indeed, if the church has failed us, if the church has been blinded and is not honestly teaching the Bible and the true *love of God*, then we need to find God elsewhere. Christians must get back to the *truth* as contained in the Scriptures—and then genuinely *practice* the truth.

CHAPTER SIX

No One Can Serve Two Masters

With the ongoing *failure* of the corporate church to meet the spiritual needs of churchgoers—and as churches increasingly misrepresent Christ and the Bible—it is time for those who *love the truth* to choose whom they will serve. Jesus gave us this profound insight: "No one is able to serve two masters; for either he will hate the one and love the other, or he will hold to the one and despise the other. You cannot serve God and mammon" (Matt. 6:24).

Are you serving two masters? Do you continue to listen to ministers and church leaders who have departed from the truth? You cannot serve God *in spirit and in truth* if you are following those who are teaching false, watered-down doctrines, religious myths, or cannot seem to move beyond mere pablum.

God has called us out of the darkness of this world into the glorious light of His truth. We are not to be conformed to the world, but transformed by the renewing of our minds (Rom. 12:1-2). This transformation is at the *heart* of the Christian calling, and cannot take place without solid, *biblical* teaching!

Those who love the world and conform to its practices—and love the "smooth things" taught by the typical Protestant pastor—cannot love God and do His will. The ways of this world are contrary to God (Rom. 8:7). God's Word commands us: "**Do not love the world, nor the things that are in the world**. If anyone loves the world, the love of the Father is not in him. Because everything that is in the world—the lust of the flesh, and the lust of the eyes, and the pretentious pride of physical life—is not from the Father, but is from the world. And the world and its lust is passing away, but the one who does the will of God abides forever" (I John 2:15-17).

But too many "Christians" *do* love this world. According to extensive research conducted over several years by the Barna Group, American Christianity is viewed as largely hypocritical. Why? As explained by David Kinnaman in his book *unChristian*, "our lives don't match our beliefs. In many ways, our lifestyles and perspectives are no different from those of anyone around us." Kinnaman says the Barna studies showed that "when it came to nonreligious factors—the substance of people's daily choices, actions, and attitudes—there were *few meaningful gaps* between born-again Christians and non-born-agains. Christians emerged as distinct in the areas people would expect—some religious activities and commitments—but not in other areas of life" (p. 46).

Kinnaman continues: "In virtually every study we conduct, representing thousands of interviews every year, born-again **Christians fail to display much attitudinal or behavioral evidence of transformed lives**. For instance, based on a study released in 2007, we found that most of the *lifestyle activities* of born-again Christians **were statistically equivalent** to those of non-born-agains.

"When asked to identify their activities over the last thirty days, born-again believers were *just as likely* to bet or gamble, to visit a pornographic Web site, to take something that did not belong to them, to consult a medium or psychic, to physically fight or abuse someone, to have consumed enough alcohol to be considered legally drunk, to have used an illegal, nonprescription drug, to have said something to someone that was not true, to have gotten back at someone for something he or she did, and to have said things behind another person's back. **No difference**" (p. 46; emphasis added).

One Barna Group study examined Americans' engagement in some type of sexually inappropriate behavior, including looking at online pornography, viewing sexually explicit magazines or movies, or having an intimate sexual encounter outside of marriage. "We found that 30 percent of born-again Christians admitted to at least one of these activities in the past thirty days, compared with 35 percent of other [non-religious] Americans. In statistical and practical terms, this means **the two groups are essentially no different** from each other." (p. 47; emphasis added).

As noted earlier, among young people, 84 percent say they personally know at least one "committed Christian." But only 15 percent thought that the lifestyle of those Christians were *significantly different* from the norm (p. 48).

Who's to blame for this dismal failure of nominal Christianity?

False teachers—those who knowingly or unknowingly teach mistruths, half-truths or outright falsehoods. Either way, churchgoers are not being taught how to *live* according to godly standards. Lives are not being transformed. But the greater problem is that churchgoers *love to have it so!* Too many people don't really want to change. The carnal, human mind is at odds with God's way of life (Rom. 8:7). Overwhelmingly, people simply don't want to give up their material and sensual pleasures.

But there are those *few* who *do* love God and His way.

If we love God and His truth, we will not tolerate false teachers who only seek to placate their congregations by teaching "smooth things." Such pastors are actually *"of the world*; because of this, they speak of the world [teach worldly things instead of the meat of God's Word], **and the world**"—those nominal "Christians" who "love to have it so" (Jer. 5:31)— **"listens to them"** (I John 4:5). But Christ declared that His followers are *not of this world*. He said in His prayer to the Father, "I have given them Your words, and the world has hated them because they are not of the world, just as I am not of the world" (John 17:14).

Think about this! If you *diligently* conform to true biblical teachings, the world *will hate you*. If you conform to the world's standards,

you will be accepted by society—but you will be conforming to the ways of the "god of this world."

The apostle James wrote that true believers *cannot be friends* with the world. He condemned those who compromised with the truth in order to conform to this world: "You adulterers and adulteresses [this includes a spiritual application, referring to the acceptance of false teachings], don't you know that the friendship [Greek *philoo*, a loving affinity as a brother] of the world is enmity with God? **Therefore whoever desires to be a friend of the world makes himself an enemy of God**" (James 4:4).

Trying to be a Christian *and* a friend of this present evil world (Gal. 1:4) is impossible—and will only result in compromising with God's Law. Jesus rebuked the church at Pergamos for this very error. In His "letter" to them, He wrote: "But I have a few things against you because you have there those who hold [observe and practice] the teaching of Balaam, who taught … the children of Israel, to eat things sacrificed to idols and to commit fornication" (Rev. 2:14). Anciently, Balaam taught Israel to *compromise* with God's Law. Thus, Jesus is warning Christians today against allowing *any* compromise with God's way of life as defined by His laws and commandments. It is interesting here that Christ mentions fornication. For the Christian today, *spiritual* fornication is any involvement with *false* religion.

Jesus continues: "Moreover, you also have those who [teach] the doctrine of the Nicolaitanes, which thing I hate" (verse 15). The Nicolaitanes were known for imposing hierarchical, dictatorial type "government" structures over their congregations.

He goes on to warn such churches: "Repent! For if you do not repent, I will come to you quickly, and will make war against [you] with the sword of My mouth. The one who has an ear, let him hear what the Spirit says to [all] the churches" (verses 16-17).

Does your church pastor fully uphold the validity of God's laws and commandments? Does he teach the Ten Commandments in an *uncompromising* manner? What is the leadership structure like in your church? Is it rigidly "top down," where no one dares question the leadership?

A true Christian cannot serve—*will not serve*—two masters! Christians need to arm themselves with "the sword of the Spirit, which is the Word of God" (Eph. 6:17). **This powerful spiritual weapon—the diligent study and reading of the Scriptures—must be utilized to defend against false teachings, watered-down doctrine, and the spirit of compromise that plagues today's "costless Christianity."** Indeed, "the Word of God is living and powerful, and sharper than any two-edged sword, piercing even to the dividing asunder of both soul and spirit, and of both the joints and the marrow, and is able to discern the thoughts and intents of the heart" (Heb. 4:12).

False Teachings Must Be *Rejected*

Paul instructed Titus, a fellow minister, to resist false doctrines and to *refute them with sound doctrine*. In his epistle to Titus, Paul wrote that a true minister of God must be "holding steadfastly to the faithful word [the truth of God], according to the teachings of Jesus Christ, [as he had been taught by the apostle Paul], so that he may be able both to **encourage with sound doctrine** and to convict those who are gainsayers. For there are many rebellious and vain talkers and deceivers, especially those from the circumcision party, whose mouths must be stopped; who are subverting whole households, teaching things which they ought not, for the sake of selfish gain…. This testimony is true. For this reason, you must rebuke them severely, that they may be sound in the faith; not paying attention to Jewish myths, and **commandments of men, which turn away from the truth**. To the pure, all things are pure; but to those who are defiled [with false doctrines] and unbelieving, nothing is pure: rather, both their minds and consciences are defiled. **They personally profess to know God, but in their works they deny Him, being abominable and disobedient** [to the Law of God], and reprobate unto every good work" (Titus 1:9-16).

It is the responsibility of every Christian who loves God and His truth to *reject* false teachings and *refute* them with the sound doctrine of Jesus Christ. But when false pastors and false ministers gain control over a church and cannot be expelled, removed or replaced with righteous teachers and ministers, then we are commanded by the Word of God to *withdraw ourselves* from them.

In his first epistle to Timothy, Paul shows that true Christians should *separate themselves* from those who do not teach and practice the true doctrine of Jesus Christ. "If anyone **teaches any different doctrine**, and *does not adhere to sound words*, even those of our Lord Jesus Christ, and the doctrine that is according to godliness [according to the truth of God], he is proud and knows nothing. Rather, he has a morbid attraction to questions and disputes over words, from which come envy, arguments, blasphemy, wicked suspicions, vain reasonings of men who have been corrupted in their minds [corrupted by philosophy and false theology], and are *destitute of the truth* [unable to teach the truth of the Bible so that people's lives are changed]—men who believe that gain [huge budgets, large congregations, outreach programs, youth programs, missions, etc.] is godliness. *From such withdraw yourself*" (I Tim. 6:3-5).

Does this description fit the congregation you attend? Does the church you attend have pretentious ministers who use lofty-sounding theological terms, but fail to make the Scriptures genuinely relevant to your life? Does your church measure spiritual standing with God by attendance figures, income, building projects, and an endless string of programs? Are false teachings being preached and accepted by your church as "official doctrines of faith"? Are the wholesome words and doctrines of Christ being replaced with half-truths? Is there real evidence of the *love of God* in your church? Are you tired of being fed spiritual pablum? Do you yearn for something more than an empty Christianity?

Yes, false ministers and false pastors have an *appearance* of godliness, and their teachings *sound* true. They call on the name of Jesus, saying, "Lord, Lord"—even proclaim Him to be the Christ (Matt. 24:5). Just as Paul wrote, they have "an outward appearance of godliness"—but they deny the power of *true* godliness (II Tim. 3:5). Paul adds, "*as for you,* **turn away from all these**"!

They "deny the power of true godliness" because the Holy Spirit of God—the very *power* that enables a Christian to live godly—does not truly work in their lives or ministries. Their ministries are virtually dead—failing to produce in their followers the real changes and growth people yearn for. Since they do not *know* the power of God's Spirit, they cannot effectively teach others to live and grow by this same power.

Paul taught only the true Gospel of Jesus Christ. He never compromised with the Word of God. He was never corrupted by the false teachers of his day. On the contrary, he vigorously opposed all such "false ministers." Every true Christian should follow the example of Paul. We should not be intimidated by false teachers, but oppose them at every turn.

CHAPTER SEVEN

Hold Fast to the Truth and Love of God

When confronted by evil forces, King David asked, "If the foundations are destroyed, what can the righteous do?" (Psa. 11:3.) This question is what many churchgoers are asking today. It is evident that the foundations of mainstream Christianity are rapidly being undermined. **What should true Christians do in these circumstances? How can we remain faithful to God?**

We must put on the whole armor of God! "Therefore, take up the whole armor of God so that **you may be able to resist in the evil day**, and having worked out all things, to *stand* [steadfast]. *Stand* therefore, having your loins girded about with *truth*, and wearing the breastplate of *righteousness*" (Eph. 6:13-14).

We must stand for the truth of God on the foundation of Christ! The true, *spiritual* church of God is to stand as the pillar and ground of God's truth in the midst of an evil and wicked generation! The apostle Paul wrote to Timothy, "These things I am writing to you, hoping to come to you shortly: but if I should delay, you have these things in writing, so that you may know how one is obligated to conduct oneself in the house of God, which is the church of the living God, **the pillar and foundation of the truth**" (I Tim. 3:14-15).

The apostle John shows us how to combat all deceivers with God's *truth* and *love*. His entire second epistle is devoted to contrasting the *truth* and the *love* of God with the "many deceivers" and their false doctrines. Here is the entire Second Epistle of John; *truth* and *love* have been highlighted in **bold type** to contrast with *deceivers* and *antichrists*.

"The elder to the chosen lady and her children, whom I **love** in **truth**, and not I alone, but also all those who have **known the truth**, for the sake of **the truth that is dwelling in us**, and shall be with us forever. Grace, mercy, and peace shall be with us from God the Father, and from the Lord Jesus Christ, the Son of the Father, **in truth and love**. I rejoiced exceedingly that I have found among your children those who are **walking in truth**, exactly as we received commandment from the Father.

And now I beseech you, lady, not as though I am writing a new commandment to you, but that which we have observed from the beginning, that **we love one another**. And **this is the love of God, that we walk according to His commandments**. This is the commandment, exactly as you heard from the beginning, that you might walk in it, because **many deceivers have entered into the world—those who do not confess that Jesus Christ has come in the flesh. This is the spirit of the deceiver and the antichrist**.

"Watch out for yourselves in order that we may not lose the things we have accomplished, but that we may receive a full reward. **Anyone who transgresses and does not continue in the doctrine of Christ does not have God. But the one who continues in the doctrine of Christ has both the Father and the Son. If anyone comes to you and does not bring this doctrine, do not receive him into your house, and do not say to him, 'Welcome!' For anyone who says 'Welcome!' to him is partaking in his evil works.**

"I have many things to write, but I do not wish to convey these things to you with paper and ink; but I hope to come to you and speak face to face in order that our joy may be completely full. The children of your chosen sister salute you. Amen."

John's admonitions make it clear that false teachers and ministers were already operating within the church while John was still alive. John clearly forbids Christians to receive any such false teachers—including those who rise up within a church. If we welcome such false ministers, we are partakers with them in their deceit. As followers of Jesus, we are to hold fast to the pure doctrines of *truth* and *love*. Again, as verse six states, "this is the **love of God**, that we **walk according to His commandments**."

Will You *Stand* for God and His Truth?

All of the original apostles stood for the *truth*—and all but John died through martyrdom. Throughout the centuries, many devout Christians have endured torturous deaths because they genuinely loved God. They never compromised with the truth for convenience or to escape persecution. If we are true Christians, we will imitate our Lord and Master, Jesus Christ, who refused to compromise with Satan and yield to his evil ways. Jesus allowed Himself to be crucified because He loved God the Father and His righteousness.

Stephen, the first true Christian martyr, refused to compromise during his trial before the Jewish Sanhedrin. After hearing his courageous testimony, the angry religious leaders stopped their ears and gnashed their teeth at him and screamed at him in a frenzy of hatred. Then they dragged him out of the city, where they had him stoned to death. What was his crime in their eyes? He refused to compromise the gospel of Christ and the truth of God by submitting to their authority and following their teachings! He preferred to die in Jesus rather than to compromise and accept their religious falsehoods and political approval.

During a time of abject apostasy and political disintegration, Asa began his righteous reign over the southern Kingdom of Judah. He demolished the idols in the land and commanded the people to seek God and to keep His commandments. For ten years, God blessed Asa and the people with rest on all sides. But when the Jews foolishly went back into idolatry, God sent a huge Ethiopian army against them. Asa turned to God for help, and Judah was victorious over their enemy.

God inspired the prophet Azariah to encourage the people: "Hear me, Asa, and all Judah and Benjamin. **The LORD is with you while you are with Him. And if you seek Him, He will be found by you**. But if you forsake Him, He will forsake you…. [Therefore] **be strong and do not let your hands be weak**, for your work shall be rewarded" (II Chron. 15:2, 7).

Then Asa and the princes and people of Judah, joined by many from the northern Kingdom of Israel, "entered into a covenant to seek the LORD God of their fathers with all their heart and with all their soul … for they had sworn with all their heart and sought Him with their whole desire. And He was found by them, and the LORD gave them rest all around" (verses 12, 15).

They put away their abominable idols and pagan gods. They returned to God and sought Him with their whole hearts. God answered and blessed them, giving them rest from their enemies.

But 36 years later, when the king of Israel came up to besiege Judah, Asa turned his back on God and made an alliance with the king of Syria (who had been a long-time enemy). In his trouble, Asa failed to look to God, thinking he could work out the problem his own way. By hiring the king of Syria to fight his battles, he compromised his standing with God. In this case, he went too far in rejecting God and did not repent. Then Hanani the seer was sent to warn Asa and pronounce God's judgment against him. Hanani told Asa, "Because you have relied on the king of Syria **and have not relied on the LORD your God**, therefore … the king of Syria has escaped out of your hand [i.e., would continue to be an ongoing source of trouble].

"Were not the Ethiopians and the Libyans a huge army [of nearly one million men] with many chariots and horsemen? Yet, because you relied on the LORD, He delivered them into your hand, for **the eyes of the LORD run to and fro in all the whole earth to show Himself strong on behalf of those whose heart is perfect toward Him**. In this you have done foolishly; therefore, from now on you shall have wars" (II Chron. 16:7-9).

Too many Christians are like Asa. They start out with great zeal for the truth of God and look to Him for strength to do His will. But after a time they grow lax and begin to compromise. When things are going well, they forget God and turn to their own devices. They put their trust in men, instead of in God. They begin to accept false teachings and pagan practices, rather than *holding fast in the truth*.

This *willingness to compromise*—by ministers *and* churchgoers— is the reason today's Christianity is in such disarray. Ministers and lay members alike are not *relying on Christ*. As a result, **too many are afraid to take a stand for the truth of God!**

But God sees our actions and knows our hearts—and expects us to *stand up* for the truth. When we do, God will be with us. He will never leave us or forsake us, as long as we are genuinely seeking His will. The psalmist asked, "Who will *rise up for me* against the evildoers? Who will *stand up for me* against the workers of iniquity?" (Psa. 94:16).

Will you make a stand for God? Will you have the courage to stand alone, if necessary? Or will you, like Asa, turn your back on God and rely on men, putting your trust in their false teachings, pablum and "smooth words"?

From the time of the early New Testament church, Christians have had to face this question. Down through the centuries, countless thousands of true Christians have been martyred because they *refused to compromise* with the truth of God. They refused to *deny* God the Father and Jesus Christ.

In light of *their* faithfulness, do you think God is obligated to give you eternal life if you compromise (or neglect) your calling, His truth and the sacrifice of Christ? Don't deceive yourself! **Christianity—or, more correctly, "Churchanity"—is in a downward spiral, headed for collapse**. Hiding your eyes from the problem won't make it go away. **If you passively sit by, if you are content with pablum and a** *costless*, **carnal-friendly "Christianity"—then you have already made your decision. You are** *compromising* **with the truth of God.**

Christians who compromise with the truth will eventually be overcome by false doctrines; they will fall into complete apostasy. If you do not *rouse yourself from spiritual apathy*, you may have to face Jesus Christ and hear Him say, "I do not know you" (see Matt. 25:1-12).

Indeed, you *must not* compromise the truth and the love of God. The Word of God clearly commands true Christians to *withdraw from fellowship* with those who would corrupt their beliefs and erode their faith—and from any church that teaches contrary to the true doctrines of Jesus Christ.

What will you do? Will you choose to be faithful to the truth of God and to love God the Father and Jesus Christ more than anyone or anything else—even if you must stand alone?

CHAPTER EIGHT

How to Know You Are Living by the *Truth*

What is the identifying *sign* and Scriptural test of a true Christian? We find the answer in Jesus' own words in the Gospel of John. Jesus declared that His true disciples are those who *continue in His teachings*. When speaking to the Jews at the temple, Jesus made it absolutely clear that His followers must remain faithful to His teachings. He said, "If you **continue** [remain and live] **in My word, you are truly My disciples**. And you shall know the truth, and **the truth shall set you free**" (John 8:31-32).

Jesus explained to the Jews that *knowing* the truth and *living by it* would set them free from the bondage of their sins. Because some did not believe, Jesus said, "Truly, truly, I say to you, everyone who practices sin is a servant [Greek, *slave*] of sin" (verse 34). Anyone who *serves sin* is a slave to sin. Who and what holds people in bondage to their sins? Satan and his lies hold them in bondage (verses 43-45). The only escape from that bondage is through Jesus Christ.

If we *live* in the truth of God, we will be free from bondage to the ways of Satan and his world. We will come to recognize Satan's lies and reject his false doctrines. Moreover, we will *know* with confidence that we are *abiding in* Jesus Christ. The apostle John wrote, "**We know that we are of God**, and that the whole world lies in the power of the wicked one. And **we know** that the Son of God has come, and has **given us an understanding, so that we may know Him Who is true**; and **we are in Him Who is true**, and in His Son, Jesus Christ. He is the true God, and the eternal life" (I John 5:19-20).

John makes it absolutely clear that those who truly know Jesus Christ will be keeping His commandments and walking as He walked. "And by this *standard* we know that we know Him: **if we keep His commandments**. The one who says, 'I know Him,' and does not keep His commandments, is a liar, and **the truth is not in him**. On the other hand, **if anyone is keeping His Word, truly in this one the love of God is being perfected. By this means we know that we are in Him**. Anyone who claims to dwell in Him is obligating himself also to walk even as He Himself walked" (I John 2:3-6).

The apostle John is here affirming Jesus' own words to the Jews at the temple. The unmistakable *sign* and *standard* that identifies true Christians is their *faithful keeping* of the commandments and teachings of Christ. When we keep Jesus' commandments and teachings, we are showing that we are led by the Holy Spirit, and we know that we are in Christ and He is in us. "And the **one who keeps His commandments** is dwelling in Him, and He in him; and by this we know that He is dwelling in us; by the Spirit which He has given to us" (I John 3:24).

We Are Sanctified Through the *Truth*

Jesus asked God the Father to sanctify every believer through His truth. He prayed, "Sanctify them in Your truth; Your Word is the truth…. And for their sakes I sanctify Myself, so that they also may be sanctified in Your truth" (John 17:17, 19).

These words of Jesus are profound! Remember, Jesus also said that He is "the Way, and the Truth, and the Life" (John 14:6). Since Jesus *is* the truth, we are sanctified in Him (I Cor. 1:2) and through His name (I Cor. 6:11) by God the Father (Jude 1).

Only through Jesus Christ can we be sanctified by the truth of God. It is through Jesus that we receive the gift of the Holy Spirit, called "the Spirit of Truth, which proceeds from the Father" (John 15:26). The Holy Spirit is the power by which God the Father and Jesus Christ are able to teach us "all things" through the Word of Truth (John 14:26). We are sealed with the Holy Spirit (II Cor. 1:22) and sanctified through the power of the Holy Spirit (Rom. 15:16).

God's Holy Spirit is called "the Spirit of Truth," not "the Spirit of half-truths." **We cannot be sanctified to the God of absolute truth, nor to Jesus Christ, Who *is* the truth, by false doctrines and half-truths. Blending falsehoods with the truth is never acceptable to God!**

Those who persistently teach falsehoods will have no part with God. Liars will be excluded from God's presence—expelled from His coming kingdom! "But the cowardly, and unbelieving, and abominable, and murderers, and fornicators, and sorcerers, and idolaters, *and all liars*, shall have their part in the lake that burns with fire and brimstone; which is the second death" (Rev. 21:8).

In Jesus' day, the religious leaders of Judaism (the scribes and Pharisees) had the truth available to them in the Scriptures. In fact, the Jewish priests and Levites were entrusted with preserving the Old Testament. More importantly, they had direct access to the truth of God in the *person* of Jesus Christ. He was the *living* Word of God, their Savior and Redeemer, dwelling among them—but they rejected Him (John 1:11).

How many times did Jesus say to the Jewish leaders, "Have you never read [in God's Word]…?" or "It is written [in Scripture]…"? But rather than believing God's Word, which is the truth, they preferred to believe and practice their *traditions*—which they held in higher esteem than the Word of God. They chose to *keep their traditions* and their positions of power rather than to humble themselves and accept the Son of God. They refused to repent, even when Jesus warned that they were actually following Satan the devil. Jesus boldly declared, "You are of your father the devil, and the lusts of your father you desire to practice. He was a murderer from the beginning, and has not stood in the truth because there is no truth in him. Whenever he speaks a lie, he is speaking from his own self: for he is a liar, and the father of it. And because I speak the truth, you do not believe Me" (John 8:44-45).

Like these Jewish leaders of old, **most modern churchgoers are following *traditions* rather than the truth**. Aren't the religious holidays of the world—Christmas, Easter, Halloween—all founded on *pagan* traditions? Along with "Sunday-keeping," these religious *traditions* are among the myths and fables Satan has used to deceive the whole world (Rev. 12:9). True Christians neither teach nor follow such myths. The apostle Peter wrote, "For we did not follow cleverly concocted myths [fables] *as our authority* when we made known to you the power and coming of our Lord Jesus Christ, but we were eyewitnesses of His magnificent glory" (II Pet. 1:16).

Herein lies the real problem with Christianity. Like the Pharisees of Jesus' day, **mainstream Christians may exhibit a *zeal* for God, but such zeal is "not according to knowledge"** (Rom. 10:2). Their zeal for Christ is based on *traditions of men*, not on the knowledge of the truth. As a feel-good religion, modern Christianity is centered largely on *emotion*, and all but denies the need for godly works, obedience and overcoming one's sinful nature. It professes to "love the Lord"—but **Jesus said that if we love Him, we will *obey* Him** (John 14:15).

Indeed, "Churchanity" clings to its myths and traditions rather than loving the truth of God. This preference for tradition and "smooth things" is a key reason the church is in such poor spiritual condition today—and ready to implode.

God Will Test You

God Himself will *test you* to see if you will abide in His truth. He must come to *know* without a doubt where each and every one of us stands. This fact is well illustrated in the book of II Chronicles, where King Hezekiah of Judah was tested **so that God could know what was "in his heart"** (II Chron. 32:31). As a righteous king, Hezekiah had done well in obeying God; and the nation of Judah was abundantly blessed as a result. But Hezekiah had a problem with pride and vanity (verses 25-26). When Babylonian ambassadors visited Judah, God used the occasion as a test—He "left [Hezekiah] **in order to try him, to know all that was in his heart**" (verse 31). But Hezekiah's pride caused him to foolishly show the inquisitive ambassadors all of his many treasures. Later, the prophet Isaiah sternly corrected Hezekiah for his grievous mistake (Isa. 39).

Likewise, God will put each of us through various circumstances to test us, to *know* all that is in our hearts. Just as He did with Abraham, God must come to say of every follower of Christ, "now I know." He must *know* that we fear and love Him (Gen. 22:12). God must test each of us in order to *know* that we will abide in His Word—*live by the truth*. But such tests need not be feared; they not only show God what is in our hearts, they also give us confidence, helping us to *know* that we are truly faithful. Indeed, your *obedience* to God's way of life will prove to Him that you are living by the truth.

Remain *Faithful* in the Truth and Love of God

The vast majority of people have been deceived into believing that their *physical presence* in worship services and their allegiance to a corporate church organization are all that is necessary for salvation. With such an approach it is easy to fall prey to false teachings, watered-down doctrines and a costless, carnal-friendly "Christianity." But God cannot be found in corporate churches and organizations. Rather, He is found by seeking His way of life in faithfulness to the truth of the Scriptures. Obedience to God's commandments is the *one*, sure way to *know* with confidence that you are *in* the truth. We must **abide and live in Christ** and **in His words** always:

> "If you **dwell in Me**, and **My words dwell in you**, you shall ask whatever you desire, and it shall come to pass for you. **In this is My Father glorified, that you bear much fruit**; so shall you be My disciples. As the Father has loved Me, I also have loved you; **live in My love. If you keep My commandments, you shall live in My love**; just as I have kept My Father's commandments and live in His love" (John 15:7-10).

Each Christian who is truly part of the greater spiritual church of God is commanded by the Word of God to make sure that he or she is *in the true faith*. "Examine yourselves to see whether you are **in the faith; prove your own selves**. Don't you of your own selves know that Jesus Christ is in you? Otherwise, you are reprobates" (II Cor. 13:5).

CHAPTER NINE

Each Christian Must *Choose*

The Word of God clearly teaches that salvation is a *gift*. Yet, each Christian is individually responsible to God to *grow* in the grace and the knowledge of Jesus Christ. We must believe the truth and *live by it*. God will not grant us salvation simply because of our physical presence within a corporate church organization.

Each Christian is responsible to work out his or her own salvation through the indwelling power of God's Holy Spirit. Paul instructed the Philippian brethren, "So then, my beloved, even as you have always obeyed, not as in my presence only, but now much more in my absence, **work out your own salvation** with fear and trembling. **For it is God Who works in you** both to will and to do according to His good pleasure" (Phil. 2:12-13).

This passage clearly shows that Christians must maintain their personal relationship with God. Every individual will have to give an account of himself or herself (Rom. 14:10; II Cor. 5:10). Never compromise your personal relationship with God for the sake of men—or for the sake of social fellowship. Remember this Christian testimony, "*It is better to live the truth alone, than to live a lie in a group*."

If you continue to fellowship in a church that teaches anything less than the whole truth of God, you are giving tacit agreement to their teachings. Paul warned, "You cannot drink the cup of the Lord, and the cup of demons. You cannot partake of the table of the Lord, and the table of demons" (I Cor. 10:21).

God Will Not Prevent Us from Choosing Evil

The history of early Christianity as recorded in the New Testament contains a valuable lesson for us today: God did not personally intervene to stop false teachings in the first century—and neither will God intervene to stop ministers and pastors from teaching falsehoods today.

Why not? From the beginning of this world, God has allowed mankind the freedom to *choose* to sin. God did not stop Adam and Eve from sinning. God did not keep Cain from killing his brother, nor did God prevent the wickedness of all mankind before the Flood. But when God did choose to intervene and execute His judgment, He sent the Flood to destroy the wicked, and spared only eight persons. God did not stop human corruption after the Flood. He did, however, confound the language of the people in order to postpone the fullness of evil until the set time in His plan.

God did not intervene to prevent the idolatry of Israel and Judah, but

He sent many prophets to warn them, calling them to repent and to return to the true God. Some of the kings and the people repented and chose to follow God. They did so by *free choice*, not because God forced them to serve Him. God forgave and blessed those who repented, and God will bless us whenever we personally choose to repent and to love and obey Him and His Son Jesus Christ. But if we choose not to repent, God *allows us* to continue in our sins.

When the leaders of a church choose to *not* repent of their false ways, God does not intervene to keep them from continuing to teach false doctrines. He simply allows them to go on practicing their error. Because they have chosen myths rather than truth, God will let them fall.

God Commands us to *Choose Life*

God is not now intervening to stop wars, famines, oppression, crime, sexual perversion, and all the evils of mankind. He has not chosen to stop these evils at this time. Rather, He has given mankind the responsibility to *choose* between good and evil.

God has given us the free moral agency to *choose*. We are blessed or cursed, and we live or die by our choices. It is God's desire that we choose to love Him and keep His commandments and live. But because God has given each individual free moral agency, each person must make his or her *own* choice.

Instead of choosing God's righteous ways, most people have chosen the easy, evil ways of Satan and the world. Those who choose to do evil will receive the wages of sin, which is death. But everyone who chooses to love God and live by His truth will receive eternal life. Here are the choices God has laid before every human being: "**Behold, I have set before you this day life and good, and death and evil**, in that I command you this day to love the LORD your God, to walk in His ways, and to keep His commandments and His statutes and His judgments so that you may live and multiply. And the LORD your God shall bless you in the land where you go to possess it [our goal is the promised Kingdom of God].

"But if your heart turn away so that you will not hear, but shall be drawn away and worship other gods and serve them, I denounce to you this day that you shall surely perish; you shall not prolong your days on the land where you pass over Jordan to go to possess it.

"I call heaven and earth to record this day against you that **I have set before you life and death, blessing and cursing. Therefore, choose life, so that both you and your seed may live**, that you may love the LORD your God, and may **obey His voice**, and may **cleave to Him**; **for He is your life and the length of your days**..." (Deut. 30:15-20).

These words, spoken by Moses to the children of Israel in Old Testament times, are especially meaningful for "spiritual Israel" today—those who are the children of Abraham through God's grace and who make up the *spiritual* Church of God. For those who are truly in the spiritual Church of God, it is time to *make a choice* between good and evil—between truth and error. Ultimately, if we do not *prove* the truth, *live by* the truth, and *defend* the truth, we will become spiritual victims—deceived into believing what others *claim* to be the truth

As we have seen, Christianity today is threatened by lukewarm "Laodicean" attitudes, inept ministers who teach nothing but pablum, and a corporate one-size-fits-all mentality that has failed to provide for the spiritual wellbeing of its followers. Within many congregations, false doctrines undermine the faith of true believers.

But make no mistake: When ministers, leaders and members *choose* to reject the truth—either deliberately or through neglect and complacency—then God allows them to follow their error. That is the lesson God teaches us throughout the Bible. God has *made each of us responsible* for his or her own choices and actions. **God will bless or curse accordingly, but He does not prevent us from choosing even error!**

In this time of increasing error and deception, we who are the *spiritual* Church of God have choices to make. Will we choose the truth of God or the myths and traditions of men? God wants to *know* what is really in our hearts. Do we truly *love* God the Father and Jesus Christ with our whole being? If we do, we *will* obey Christ: "If you love Me, keep the commandments—namely, My commandments" (John 14:15). Do we truly love His Word, which He has so wonderfully preserved for us? Do we exemplify the *love of God* in our daily lives? Do we really want to inherit the Kingdom of God and live with God the Father and Jesus Christ for all eternity?

To those churchgoers who would be His *true* followers, Jesus made it absolutely clear that the stakes were high and the way was difficult. He said, "Enter in through the narrow gate; for **wide is the gate and broad is the way that leads to destruction**, and **many are those who enter through it**; for **narrow is the gate and difficult is the way that leads to life**, and **few are those who find it**" (Matt. 7:13-14).

Jesus describes the single-minded devotion that is required of a *true* Christian: "If anyone comes to Me and does not hate [or, *love less* by comparison] his father, and mother, and wife, and children, and brothers and sisters, and, in addition, his own life also, he cannot be My disciple. And whoever does not carry his [own] cross [make whatever sacrifice necessary] and come after Me cannot be My disciple" (Luke 14:26-27). Jesus emphasized this truth when He said, "The one who loves father or mother *more than Me* is not worthy of Me: and the one who loves son or daughter *more than Me* is not worthy of Me. And the one who *does not take up his cross and follow Me* is not worthy of Me" (Matt. 10:37-38).

As these passages clearly show, the true Christian can put *nothing* before God—not even family. We must "take up our cross"—do *whatever* is necessary to follow Christ into the Kingdom of God. And this includes seeking and adhering to the *truth* of the Bible—or we are not worthy of Jesus.

Each of us is personally responsible to God the Father and Jesus Christ for his or her own actions and beliefs. We are being judged individually by God according to our faith and our conduct. God commands us to love Him wholeheartedly and live by His every Word. If we stray from God and begin to believe and practice error, God will make us aware of our sins in the hope that we may repent and have our sins blotted out by the blood of Jesus Christ (I John 1:6-2:2). But God will not stop us from sinning—not even if we are a top leader or minister in a corporate church organization. Those ministers who choose to preach pablum, tradition or outright error will be warned by God to repent—but God will not stop them if they choose to follow deception and apostasy!

We Must Accept Our Personal Responsibility

In today's world, people readily blame others for their irresponsibility and their lack of character and self-control. They often blame society, or their mother or father, or their boss, or the government, or others in positions of authority. Because people do not want to accept personal responsibility for their own sins and actions, they try to place the blame on others. That is exactly what Adam and Eve did after they sinned. Such excuses have no standing before God and cannot release anyone from his or her personal accountability to God.

Unfortunately, when ministers and church leaders sin by complacency, negligence or by accepting and teaching error, the brethren suffer by becoming confused, deceived or lulled into a spiritual stupor.

If your church has reached this condition, it is important to remember that **every Christian is personally accountable to God to continually be studying the Word and to "prove all things"** (I Thess. 5:21). We cannot blame others for deceiving us if we fail to lay a solid foundation in the Word of God. God has given each Christian the personal responsibility to *hold fast to the truth*, to grow in grace and knowledge, to follow that which is good, and to love Him with all the heart, with all the mind, with all the soul and with all the strength. Ultimately, each one of us will be required to **stand before the judgment seat of Christ to give an account of what we did with the truth of God**.

CHAPTER TEN

Every Christian Must Defend the Truth

What is our Christian duty before God when we hear false doctrines being preached? Should we submit to church leaders who, in ignorance, promote false teachings that deny Christ? Are we to remain silent while ministers and brethren alike are swept into spiritual error? What did first-century Christians do when the churches of God were confronted with error and deception?

The apostle Jude wrote to faithful Christians of his day, encouraging them to stand up against apostasy. Jude addressed his epistle to the "called saints"—all who were called by God the Father to receive salvation through Christ. His letter warns of a subtle conspiracy by false teachers working within the churches in an attempt to pervert the true teachings of the Scriptures. Jude admonishes every Christian to defend the true doctrines delivered by Jesus and taught by His apostles.

Jude's letter deals strongly with false teachers—declaring that such teachers are *not* led by the Spirit of God, but are, in some cases, actually motivated by satanic powers (verse 19). He exhorts us to help our brethren who are being caught up in deception and apostasy (verses 22-23). Jude's words clearly show that Christians have a *personal responsibility* to witness to their fellow brethren to save them from spiritual destruction.

The Epistle of Jude

"Jude, a servant of Jesus Christ and brother of James, to the called saints, sanctified by God the Father and kept in Jesus Christ: mercy and peace and love be multiplied to you. Beloved, when personally exerting all my diligence to write to you concerning the common salvation, I was compelled to write to you, **exhorting you to fervently fight for the faith**, which once for all time has been delivered to the saints. For **certain men have stealthily crept in**, those who long ago have been written about, condemning them to this judgment. **They are ungodly men, who are perverting the grace of our God, turning it into licentiousness, and are personally denying the only Lord God and our Lord Jesus Christ.**

"But I myself want to remind you, though you once understood this, that the Lord, after saving a people out of the land of Egypt, the second time destroyed those who did not believe. And the angels who did not keep their own original

43

domain, but deserted their habitation, He is holding in eternal bonds under darkness unto the judgment of the great day. Just as Sodom and Gomorrah—and the cities surrounding them, in the same manner as them—having given themselves over to sexual debaucheries, and having gone after different flesh, are themselves exhibited as a perpetual example of undergoing the punishment of eternal fire,

"In the same way also, these dreamers of filthy dreams are defiling the flesh, and are declaring as invalid the lordship of God, and are blaspheming the divine powers. But Michael the archangel, when he was personally taking issue with the devil, disputing about the body of Moses, did not presume to pronounce a reviling judgment against him, but said, 'The Lord Himself rebuke you!' As for these, whatever things they do not understand, they blaspheme; but whatever things they understand by instinct, as irrational brute beasts, they are corrupting themselves in these things.

"Woe to them! For they have walked in the way of Cain; and for gain, they have wholly given themselves up to Balaam's delusion, and have perished in the rebellion of Korah. These are subversive stains in your love feasts, feasting in person together with you; fearlessly they are feeding themselves. They are clouds without water, being driven by the winds; trees of late autumn, without any fruit, uprooted, twice dead; raging waves of the sea, casting up like foam their own ignominious shame; wandering stars, for whom has been reserved the blackest darkness forever!

"And Enoch, the seventh from Adam, also prophesied of these, proclaiming, 'Behold, the Lord comes with ten thousands of His holy saints to execute judgment against all, and to convict all who are ungodly of all their works of evil ungodliness that they have impiously committed, and of all the hard things that ungodly sinners have spoken against Him.' These are complainers and critics, who are walking after their own personal lusts, while their mouths are speaking great swelling words, flattering persons for the sake of advantage.

"But you, beloved, remember the words that were spoken before by the apostles of our Lord Jesus Christ; because they said to you that **in the last time there would be mockers, who would be selfishly walking according to their own ungodly lusts. These are the ones who cause division; they are [using] psychic [powers], not having the Spirit of God.**

"But you, beloved, **be building up yourselves on your most holy faith, praying in the Holy Spirit**, so that you **keep**

yourselves in the love of God while you are personally **awaiting the mercy of our Lord Jesus Christ unto eternal life**.

"Now on the one hand, **show mercy to those individuals who are doubting; but on the other hand, save others with fear, snatching them out of the fire**, hating even the garment that has been defiled by the flesh.

"Now **to Him Who is able to keep them from falling, and to bring them into the presence of His own glory, blameless in exceeding joy**, to the only wise God our Savior, be the glory and greatness, the might and authority, even now, and into all the ages of eternity. Amen."

We Must Individually Defend the Truth

Jude's inspired words reveal that we are *individually responsible* as Christians to show brethren who are being deceived by false teachers that their ways are contrary to the Scriptures. We are to plead with our brethren, that they turn from their error and repent—and withdraw from any church that does not rightly preach the Bible.

Indeed, those who truly desire to walk in the light of God's Word can *have no spiritual fellowship* with those who insist on following after "costless Christianity." God commands true believers to separate themselves from the falsehoods and sinful practices of "Babylon the Great"—*false religion*. In the book of Revelation we read, "Come out of her, My people, so that you do not take part in her sins, and that you do not receive of her plagues, for her sins have reached as far as heaven, and God has remembered her iniquities. Render to her as she has rendered to you; and give to her double, even according to her works. In the cup that she mixed, give her back double!" (Rev. 18:4-6.)

Those who worship God in spirit and in truth (John 4:23-24) can have nothing to do with false "Christianity." True believers cannot fellowship with those who persistently teach myths, human traditions, outright error—or those who cannot progress beyond pablum. **Today, "Churchanity" has overwhelmingly become *costless*, carnal-friendly "Christianity"— which is false religion. If we accept such teachings and practices, we are in danger of forfeiting our eternal life!**

God has made it His responsibility to bring us to salvation through Jesus, to give us His Spirit, to give us understanding, to fill us with His love, *if we hunger and thirst for it*. But God does not personally intervene to keep us from being exposed to false doctrines. Instead, He has given us the truth of His Word so that we may recognize and refute false doctrines. He has provided "the Spirit of the truth" to guide us and to teach us the truth of all things pertaining to eternal life through Christ. We will not be deceived by false doctrines if we are *earnestly studying* and *seeking the truth* of God's

Word with the help of God's Holy Spirit. Although we will not understand everything perfectly, we will be growing in the grace and the knowledge of our Lord Jesus Christ.

As individual Christians, we must be grounded and built up in the Word of God in order to resist the corrupting influence of false ministers. It is our *individual Christian responsibility* to diligently study the Word of God in order to discern truth from error, lest we too be deceived.

In the book of Hebrews, Paul admonishes the brethren because they were lax and negligent in their personal Christian responsibility. These Christians were spiritually immature in their understanding because they had not been diligently grounding themselves in the Word of God. Paul declared, "For truly, by this time you ought to be teachers, but instead you need to have someone teach you again what are the beginning principles of the oracles of God, and have become those in need of milk, and not of solid food. For everyone who is partaking of milk is **unskilled in the word of righteousness** because he is an infant. But solid food is for those who are fully grown [spiritually mature], **who through repeated practice have had their senses trained to discern between good and evil**" (Heb. 5:12-14).

It is God's purpose to bring us to spiritual maturity, fully conforming us to the perfect character of Jesus Christ, so that we also may be born into His divine family and be His children forever. But we cannot become spiritually mature if we continue to attend dead or dying churches, feeding only on pablum—or worse, outright error.

Rather, we must earnestly seek to understand the *full truth* of God's Word, that we may grow spiritually. Only then will we be able to "discern between good and evil"—and be able to recognize and refute false doctrines.

True Fellowship Is with God the Father and Jesus Christ

True Christian fellowship begins with a personal relationship with God and Christ through the power of the Holy Spirit. The apostle John wrote, "That which we have seen and have heard we are reporting to you in order that you also may have fellowship with us; for the fellowship— indeed, **our fellowship—is with the Father and with His own Son, Jesus Christ**" (I John 1:3).

We must "worship God in spirit and in truth" because God is Spirit. True spiritual fellowship is not a once-a-week event, but an ongoing *relationship* with God and Jesus as we seek daily to live by every word of God. Jesus said, "It is written, 'Man shall not live by bread alone, but by every word that proceeds out of the mouth of God' " (Matt. 4:4).

Fellowship with God the Father and Jesus Christ cannot be granted by any church organization. Such fellowship is based on the personal covenant with God that every true believer enters into at baptism. While this intimate spiritual fellowship is God's gift to every Christian, it is *our responsibility* to maintain that fellowship by continuing to walk in the light of His

Word—for only then are we truly in spiritual union with God the Father and Jesus Christ.

If we continue in this true fellowship, we need have no fear. God will not forsake us as long as we remain faithful to His truth. If we *defend the truth*, we may have to stand alone for a while, but we will always have fellowship with the Father and Jesus Christ. When a few brethren are able to fellowship and study God's Word together, *God will be with them.* Jesus has promised that wherever two or three *genuine* believers are gathered in His name, He will be in their midst (Matt. 18:20).

Will You be Numbered Among the Faithful?

Every true Christian is being tried and tested to see if he or she truly loves God the Father and Jesus Christ. He said, "**The one who has My commandments and is keeping them, that is the one who loves Me**; and the one who loves Me shall be loved by My Father, and I will love him and will manifest Myself to him.... **If anyone loves Me, he will keep My word**; and My Father will love him, and We will come to him and make Our abode with him. **The one who does not love Me does not keep My words**; and the word that you hear is not Mine, but the Father's Who sent Me" (John 14:21, 23-24).

Jesus has given us the true doctrines of God. If we love Him, we will *remain steadfast in His teachings*, knowing that we are building our lives upon the only sure foundation. Paul shows that we can only receive the gift of eternal life by building upon the foundation laid by Christ. "For no one is able to lay any other foundation besides that which has been laid, which is Jesus Christ. Now if anyone builds upon this foundation gold, silver, precious stones, wood, hay or stubble, the work of each one shall be manifested; for the day of trial will declare it, because it shall be revealed by fire; and the fire shall prove what kind of work each one's is. If the work that anyone has built endures, he shall receive a reward. If the work of anyone is burned up, he shall suffer loss, but he himself shall be saved, yet as through fire" (I Cor. 3:11-15).

As Paul wrote, Christians are now being *judged* on how we are building upon the foundation of Christ. God will not give us an eternal reward if we are not building the *true works of righteousness* that will withstand the fiery trials He allows to test us.

The apostle Peter also warned that Christians will face difficult trials: "**Beloved, do not be surprised at the fiery trial among you which is taking place to test you, as if some strange thing were happening to you**. But to the degree that you have a share in the sufferings of Christ, rejoice; so that, at the revelation of His glory, you also may rejoice exceedingly. If you are reviled for the name of Christ, you are blessed because the Spirit of glory and the Spirit of God is resting upon you; on their part He is blasphemed, but on your part He is glorified.

"Assuredly, let none of you suffer as a murderer, or a thief, or an evil doer, or as an overlording busybody in other people's lives. Yet if anyone is suffering as a Christian, he should not be ashamed, but let him glorify God because of this, for **the time has come for judgment to begin with the household of God**; and if it first begins with us, what will be the end of those who do not obey the gospel of God? And if the righteous are saved with much difficulty, what will become of the ungodly and the sinner? For this reason also, let those who suffer according to the will of God commit their souls to Him in well doing, as to a faithful Creator" (I Pet. 4:12-19).

Peter tells us not to be discouraged or disheartened by these fiery trials. We must allow nothing to persuade us to turn aside from following Jesus Christ. If we suffer because we choose to remain faithful to His teachings, we will be richly rewarded at His coming. Let us rejoice in this eternal promise!

Are you willing to follow the example of Christ by remaining faithful to the truth of God, even if it brings persecution from your closest friends and members of your own family? Are you willing to hold fast to the true teachings of the Bible, even if it means you must withdraw from fellowship with your present church organization? Is your membership in a corporate church more important than worshipping God in *spirit* and in *truth*?

Remember, the very **love of God**—which is based on the truth of His Word—is to be *perfected* in genuine Christians: "And we have known and have believed the love that God has toward us. God is love, and the one who dwells in love is dwelling in God, and God in him. By this spiritual indwelling, **the love of God is perfected within us, so that we may have confidence in the day of judgment** because even as He is, so also are we in this world. There is no fear in the love of God; rather, perfect love casts out fear because fear has torment. And the one who fears has not been made perfect in the love of God. We love Him because He loved us first" (I John 4:16-19).

CHAPTER ELEVEN

What God Requires of Ministers

God is continually trying and testing every minister and pastor to determine who truly loves Him and His Word. In fact, God is making a distinction between those ministers who faithfully preach His Word in *truth* and those who, in complacency and neglect, fail to provide for the spiritual needs of their congregations. God is also taking note of those who are only seeking position, prestige and power.

Every minister of Jesus Christ needs to carefully examine his own heart and mind to *honestly evaluate* his personal *motives* for being in the ministry. This is the self-examination that Christ required the apostle Peter to undergo. Every minister should apply this same scriptural test to himself:

> "Therefore, when they had finished eating, Jesus said to Simon Peter, 'Simon, son of Jonas, do you love Me more than these [the other apostles and disciples]?' And he said to Him, 'Yes, Lord. You know that I love You.' He said to him, '**Feed My lambs!**'

> "He said to him again a second time, 'Simon, son of Jonas, do you love Me?' And he said to Him, 'Yes, Lord. You know that I love You.' He said to him, '**Shepherd My sheep!**'

> "He said to him the third time, 'Simon, son of Jonas, do you love Me?' Peter was grieved because He said to him the third time, 'Do you love Me?' And he said to Him, 'Lord, You know all things. You know that I love You.' Jesus said to him, '**Feed My sheep!**' " (John 21:15-17).

Each minister who has the Spirit of God has been entrusted with this commission, just as Jesus charged Peter. Each minister needs to know that the very purpose of his calling is to *feed the sheep of God*—the brethren of Jesus Christ. If any man is a minister for *any* other reason, his ministry will be shallow and ineffective.

Those ministers who *truly love Jesus* will faithfully continue to **preach the whole truth of God** even at the risk of personal loss and deprivation, just as Paul instructed Timothy:

> "And that from a child you have known the Holy Writings, which are able to make you wise unto salvation through faith, which *is* in Christ Jesus. All Scripture *is* God-breathed and *is*

profitable for doctrine, for conviction, for correction, for instruction in righteousness; so that the man of God may be complete, fully equipped for every good work.... **I charge you, therefore, in the sight of God, even the Lord Jesus Christ**, Who is ready to judge *the* living and *the* dead at His appearing and His kingdom: **Preach the Word! Be urgent in season and out of season; convict, rebuke, encourage, with all patience and doctrine**" (II Tim. 3:15-17; 4:1-2).

Every minister, pastor and teacher will follow the example of Paul, who faithfully taught the true Gospel message because he valued the *spiritual welfare* of his brethren above his own physical life. Paul endured great persecution and hardship as he faithfully taught his brethren the truth of God that leads to eternal life. Here are Paul's heartfelt words to his Corinthian brethren:

"For those of us [ministers] who are living are always [continually] delivered to death for Jesus' sake, that the life of Jesus may also be manifested in our mortal flesh. So then, on the one hand, death is working in us [ministers]; and on the other hand, life is working in you [brethren].... For **all things are for your sakes**, so that the abounding grace may cause the thanksgiving of many to overflow unto the glory of God.

"For this reason, we do not lose heart; but if our outward man is being brought to decay, yet the inward man is being renewed day by day. For the momentary lightness of our tribulation is working out for us an immeasurably greater and everlasting fullness of glory. While we consider not the things that are seen [the tribulations and difficulties], but the things that are not seen [eternal life]. For the things that are seen are temporary, but the things that are not seen are eternal" (II Cor. 4:11-18).

The apostle Paul was *faithful* to the charge that he received from Christ. As a true minister of God, he *fed the flock* with the pure doctrines of the Word of God. His reward is sure! Paul will inherit eternal life with glory and power in the Kingdom of God, serving the Father and Jesus Christ in eternal love! This is the reward that God offers to every minister who faithfully preaches the *pure truth* of His Word, regardless of corporate organization or church affiliation.

Ministers and Pastors to Face Harsher Judgment

Without exception, every minister of Christ will be **judged according to his works**. If he is faithfully preaching the *truth* of God without compromise, he will receive an eternal reward. However, if he is *compromising with the truth* in order to protect his position, his prestige, his salary or his pension, he will have to give an account to Christ. In fact, James warns that those in positions of spiritual leadership will face a stricter judgment: "My brethren, do not many of you become teachers, knowing that **we will receive more severe judgment**" (James 3:1).

Ironically, the majority of today's "Christian" ministers do not truly *believe* the Scriptures—and thus do not *obey* what God commands. Jesus foretold of this very condition among "religious leaders":

> "Not everyone who says to Me, 'Lord, Lord,' shall enter into the kingdom of heaven; but the one who is doing the will of My Father, Who is in heaven. **Many [pastors and ministers] will say to Me in that day** [of judgment, when everyone—*including religious leaders*—will come before the judgment seat of Christ to give an account], 'Lord, Lord, **did we not prophesy [teach or minister] through Your name?** And *did we not* cast out demons through Your name? And *did we not* perform many works of power through Your name?' **And then [because of their works] I will confess to them, 'I never knew you. Depart from Me, you who work lawlessness'** " (Matt. 7:21-23).

Indeed, many ministers and pastors go before their congregations using Christ's name—saying, "Lord" *this* and "Lord" *that*. Yet, because they don't truly *believe* what the Bible says, they teach fables and traditions of men. To make them palatable, such teachings are often cloaked in analogies or "human interest" stories.

Jesus will have no choice but to say to them, "I don't know you"—because their whole "Christian experience" is based on ideas of men, not on sound biblical doctrine. As Paul wrote, they have "an outward appearance of godliness, but [are guilty of] denying the power of *true* godliness" (II Tim. 3:5). The "power of true godliness" lies in *heartfelt obedience* to the laws and commandments of God, made possible by the indwelling of the Holy Spirit. But a humble belief in the absolute authority of the Scriptures—both Old and New Testaments—is the starting point.

In fact, mainstream pastors and ministers typically do not use the *entire* Bible; they lean heavily on Paul's writings while almost totally avoiding the Old Testament. **This always leads to gross doctrinal error**. The end result is *spiritual blindness*—a make-believe reality, an illusion. The average Christian simply does not realize that Satan the devil is actively deceiving the *whole world* (Rev. 12:9) through both government and *religious* leaders.

Many of today's "Christian" pastors and ministers are responsible for carelessly deluding their followers into accepting a no-works, no-cost, carnal-friendly "Christianity" that leaves them unsatisfied and spiritually empty. The prophet Isaiah warned of just such a condition:

> "It shall even be as when a hungry one dreams, and behold, he eats, but he awakes and **his soul is empty**; or as when a thirsty man dreams, and behold, he drinks; but he awakes, and behold, *he is* faint and **his soul is longing**…. [They think they are being fed spiritually, but are actually starving.] Be stunned and amazed! Blind your eyes and be blind! They are [spiritually] drunk, but not with wine; they stagger, but not *with* strong drink, for [because of your unbelief and disobedience] the LORD has poured out upon you the spirit of deep sleep, and has closed your eyes [spiritual ignorance and blindness]; He has covered [made blind] the prophets [pastors and ministers] and your rulers, *and* the seers. And the vision of all has become to you like the words of a book that is sealed, which they give to one who is learned saying, 'Please read this,' and he says, 'I cannot, for it is sealed.' And the book is delivered to him who is not learned, saying, 'Please read this,' and he says, 'I am not learned.' [The Scriptures are *closed* to them because of their lack of genuine obedience.] [And what is the CAUSE of this condition?] And the LORD said, '**Because this people draws near *Me* with their mouth, and with their lips honor Me** [they use all the right-sounding "religious" phrases], **but their worship of Me is made up of the traditions of men learned by rote, and their fear** [and obedience] **toward Me is *taught* by the commandments of men**' " (Isa. 29:8-13).

This key passage is a powerful indictment against today's "Christianity"! Yes, men desire to *be religious*—to give "lip service" to God—while delighting in their *own* works and traditions. Overwhelmingly, this world's ministers and pastors have convinced themselves that God approves of their ways—even when they *know* many "Christian" practices (such as Sunday worship and the popular holidays of Easter and Christmas) are actually pagan and contrary to the Word of God.

Because of such irresponsible compromising with the Scriptures, **God blinds their eyes and understanding**. Notice verse 14: "Therefore, behold, I will proceed to do again a marvelous work among this people, *even* a marvelous work and a wonder, for the wisdom of their wise ones [their pastors and ministers] shall perish, and the wisdom of their intelligent ones [their scholars and theologians] shall vanish"—and, thus, they become *fools* (Rom. 1:19-22).

Religious leaders who compromise with the truth become blind to the true plan of God. Paul writes: "But if our gospel is hidden, it is hidden to those who are perishing; in whom **the god of this age has blinded the minds of those who do not believe**…" (II Cor. 4:3-4). In *unbelief*, they do not genuinely obey God's laws and commandments. Thus, they are blinded—an automatic spiritual penalty for disobedience.

To *Knowingly* Teach False Doctrine Is Willful Sin

While the majority of "Christian" pastors and ministers are, without a doubt, *sincere* in their beliefs and convinced they are correct, there are "wolves in sheep's clothing" who are bent on *deliberate* deception. In fact, such religionists twist and distort God's word in rebellion—denying the true way of life described in the Scriptures. Of them Isaiah says, "**Woe** *to* those who go deep to hide *their* [secret] purpose from the LORD! And their works are in the dark, and they say, 'Who sees us? And who knows us?' Surely, **you have turned things upside down!** Shall the potter be regarded as the potter's clay; for shall the work say of him who made it, 'He did not make me?' Or shall the thing formed say to him who formed it, 'He had no understanding?' " (Isa. 29:15-16).

Likewise, the prophet Ezekiel exposes the schemes of those pastors and ministers who would *knowingly* undermine the truth.

> "**There is a conspiracy of her prophets** in her midst, like a roaring lion tearing the prey. They have devoured souls; they have taken the treasure and precious things; they made many widows in her midst. **Her priests have done violence to My law** [claiming that it has been abolished] **and have profaned My holy things. They have put no difference between the holy and the profane, and have not taught the difference between the unclean and the clean, and THEY HAVE HIDDEN THEIR EYES FROM MY SABBATHS, and I am profaned among them**…. And her prophets have covered themselves *with* whitewash, **seeing false visions and divining lies unto them, saying, 'Thus says the Lord GOD' when the LORD has not spoken**" (Ezek. 22:25-26, 28).

God does not view this as simple *ignorance* or a lack of knowledge by religious leaders. He declares it for what it truly is—*a deliberate conspiracy!* God has made it quite *plain* in the Bible how He expects men to live. But many of today's ministers and pastors have *closed their eyes* to the truth.

For example, the majority of Orthodox Christendom *knows* that the observance of Sunday is nowhere sanctioned in the Bible—that it is of *pagan* origin. But too many ministers and pastors willingly continue in the charade that it is an "authorized Christian practice"—authorized by *men*. They have deluded themselves (and their congregations) that Sunday worship is "sanctioned" by God. But to them God says: "What right have you to declare My statutes, and to take up My covenant in your mouth? [Again, they love to say "Lord, Lord" and sound religious.] Yea, [but in reality] **you hate to be taught, and you cast My words behind you**" (Psa. 50:16-17).

Similarly, Isaiah describes those religious leaders who knowingly mix error with truth:

> "**Woe to those who draw iniquity with cords of vanity**, and sin with cart ropes; who [disingenuously] say, 'Let Him hurry *and* hasten His work, so that we may see it; and let the purpose of the Holy One of Israel draw near and come, so that we may know!' **Woe to those who call evil good and good evil; who put darkness for light and light for darkness; who put bitter for sweet and sweet for bitter**!

> "**Woe unto *them that are* wise in their own eyes**, and prudent in their own sight! **Woe** unto *them that are* mighty to drink wine, and men of strength to mingle strong drink; who justify the wicked for a bribe, and **take away the righteousness of the righteous from him**! Therefore as the fire devours the stubble, and the flame burns up the chaff; their root shall be like rottenness, and their blossoms shall go up like dust because **they have cast away the law of the LORD of hosts, and despised the Word of the Holy One of Israel. Therefore, the anger of the LORD is kindled against His people**, and He has stretched out His hand against them, and has stricken them…. In all this His anger is not turned away, but His hand is stretched out still" (Isa. 5:18-25).

So much of what is wrong with mainstream "Christianity" is the result of its leaders *rejecting* the Word of God in favor of human tradition. But if pastors and ministers would *honestly* and *humbly* search the Word of God—and put it above any and all traditions—they could begin to understand the truth.

Paul's inspired message to the Hebrew Christians is a timeless warning to all who *turn away* from the truth and begin to believe or teach false doctrines. As Paul pointed out to these early Christians, to knowingly turn away from the truth and accept false doctrines that deny Christ is *willful sin* and will bring God's just retribution. *How much more so for those who claim to be ministers of the Gospel!*

He declared, "For if we **willfully go on sinning after receiving the knowledge of the truth**, there is no longer any sacrifice for sins, but a terrifying expectation of inevitable judgment and of fierce fire, which will devour the adversaries of God. Consider this: anyone who rejects the law of Moses dies without mercy under the testimony of two or three witnesses.

"How much worse punishment do you think he will deserve who has **trampled underfoot the Son of God**, and has regarded the blood of the covenant, with which he was sanctified, *as* an unholy thing, and has scorned the Spirit of grace?

"For we know Him Who has said, 'Vengeance belongs to Me, I will recompense,' says the Lord. And again, 'The Lord will judge His people.' It is a fearful thing to fall into the hands of the living God" (Heb. 10:26-31).

No minister or pastor can afford to ignore this solemn warning! If we deny Jesus Christ and the truth by *knowingly* teaching false doctrines, we are removing ourselves from God's grace and are placing ourselves under His judgment! It is a fearful thing to face the judgment of the living God and the prospect of eternal death! Far better to humbly repent and seek God's mercy and grace before it is too late.

Those who do not repent of their unfaithfulness are in danger of becoming *hardened* in their own deception. Paul warned, "Beware, brethren, lest perhaps there be in any of you an evil heart of unbelief, **in apostatizing from the living God**. Rather, be encouraging one another each day, while it is called 'today,' so that none of you become **hardened by the deceitfulness of sin**. For we are companions of Christ, if we truly hold the confidence that we had at the beginning steadfast until the end. As it is being said, 'Today, if you will hear His voice, do not harden your hearts, as in the rebellion' " (Heb. 3:12-15).

When those who once believed the truth become fully hardened in their hearts, they are no longer convicted by the Spirit to seek repentance. There remains no more grace for them, but only the judgment of God. Just as God destroyed those who sinned in the provocation in the wilderness, God will destroy all sinners who will not hear His Word and who despise the Spirit of grace.

Compromising Ministers Must Repent!

If you—as an elder, minister or teacher—have been compromising the truth of God, watering down Scripture, or preaching "smooth things" in order to remain in good standing in an organized church, *you are in great spiritual danger!* To whom much is given, *much is required* (Luke 12:48)! The Word of God clearly shows that a Christian who *knowingly* condones sin and error is defiling his or her conscience. A defiled conscience will eventually grow calloused and indifferent to the convicting power of the Holy Spirit.

Paul describes the end result of yielding to the pressure and temptation to teach false doctrines: "Now the Spirit tells us explicitly that in the latter times **some shall apostatize from the faith**, and shall **follow deceiving spirits** and doctrines of demons; **speaking lies in hypocrisy**, their consciences having been cauterized [as if] with a hot iron" (I Tim. 4:1-2).

Every "Christian" teacher who has yielded to false teachings is in danger of ending up in this unregenerate spiritual condition. **It is the continued condoning and acceptance of sin and error that leads to loss of salvation**. Opposing false doctrines—even when they are promoted by church "authorities"—will never cause a Christian to lose his or her salvation.

If you have been compromising the truth by accepting or teaching false doctrines, you need to *repent* and *return to God*—for He will cleanse each one who truly repents with humble supplications. Only then can you be restored in love and faith to God the Father and grow in the grace and knowledge of our Lord Jesus Christ.

Importantly, do not *wait* on a "general movement" toward repentance among churchgoers! Such a movement will almost certainly never come. It is a grave mistake to delay our personal repentance when the Holy Spirit convicts us of sin and error in our lives!

David, a man after God's own heart, was *wholehearted* in his repentance when the Spirit of God convicted him. When David had sinned greatly against God, this was his prayer of repentance: "LORD, be gracious unto me; **heal my soul, for I have sinned against You**" (Psa. 41:4). Again, when repenting of his adultery with Bathsheba and the killing of Uriah her husband, he pleaded:

> "Have mercy upon me, O God, according to Your loving-kindness; according to the greatness of Your compassion, blot out my transgressions. **Wash me thoroughly from my iniquity, and cleanse me from my sin**, for I acknowledge my transgressions, and my sin is ever before me.
>
> "Against You, You only, have I sinned, and done evil in Your sight, that You might be justified when You speak and be in the right when You judge. Behold, I was brought forth in iniquity, and in sin did my mother conceive me.
>
> "Behold, **You desire truth in the inward parts**; and in the hidden part You shall make me to know wisdom. **Purge me with hyssop, and I shall be clean; wash me, and I shall be whiter than snow**. Make me to hear joy and gladness that the bones which You have broken may rejoice.
>
> "**Hide Your face from my sins, and blot out all my iniquities. Create in me a clean heart**, O God, and **renew a steadfast spirit within me**. Cast me not away from Your presence, and take not Your Holy Spirit from me" (Psa. 51:1-11).

Any minister or pastor who has sinned against God by compromising with the truth needs to have David's attitude of deep repentance and humility. Such a person needs to ask God to *cleanse his heart* from the sins of neglect, apathy, compromise, complacency, ineptness—or of *knowingly* casting aside the truth of God and teaching falsehoods! Ask God to *heal your mind and heart*—for He will hear and He will answer.

Jesus gave this sobering admonition to the church at Laodicea—though the warning is applicable to *all* churches: "I counsel you to buy from

Me gold purified by fire so that you may be rich; and white garments so that you may be clothed, and the shame of your nakedness may not be revealed; and to anoint your eyes with eye salve, so that you may see!

"As many as I love, I rebuke and chasten. Therefore, **be zealous and repent**. Behold, I stand at the door and knock. If anyone hears My voice and opens the door, I will come in to him, and will sup with him, and he with Me.

"To the one who overcomes will I give authority to sit with Me in My throne, even as I also overcame, and sat down with My Father in His throne. **The one who has an ear, let him hear what the Spirit says to the churches**" (Rev. 3:18-22).

May God grant you the ears to hear, the heart to repent, and the courage to stand for the truth. May God grant you the understanding and strength you need to fulfill your personal, sacred duty as a minister to *defend the faith* once delivered to the saints.

CHAPTER TWELVE

The Approaching Great Apostasy

The New Testament clearly shows that false teachers were working *within* the church while the original apostles were still alive. Such counterfeit ministers were wrongly handling the Word of God, resulting in teachings that *sounded* good, cloaked in clever theological terminology, but were nevertheless *false*. Ultimately, whether intentional or unintentional, such deceitful teachings originate from the spiritual darkness of Satan the devil.

Widespread deception is now taking place in modern "Churchanity." Those behind such deception, knowingly or unknowingly, are drawing from the original source of all false religion—"Babylon the Great, the Mother of Harlots and the Abominations of the Earth." While such false teachers—in ignorance or willful determination—proclaim Satan's ancient fables as "enlightenment," they are leading millions of churchgoers into spiritual darkness.

Many Christians in New Testament times failed to heed the warnings of Christ and His apostles against deceivers who would bring in false doctrines. After the death of the apostles, the subversion of the church began to accelerate. In his book *The Story of the Christian Church*, Jesse Lyman Hurlbut wrote of the vast, rapid changes that took place in the church at that time. "We name the last generation of the first century, from 68 to 100 AD, 'The Age of Shadows.'... For fifty years after St. Paul's life, a curtain hangs over the church, through which we strive vainly to look; and when at last it rises about 120 AD with the writings of the earliest church fathers, we find a church in many aspects *very different* from that in the days of St. Peter and St. Paul" (p. 42).

The changes to the apostolic church were so swift, so complete and so thorough that the church became almost unrecognizable. Whole churches were overcome by the spiritual darkness of false doctrines. The overwhelming majority of Christians were deceived into accepting "new" doctrines; those who refused were looked upon as heretics. Christians who were faithful to the true Gospel of Jesus Christ were *driven out of the local churches* (III John). They left the "organizations of men" in order to love and serve God in the *truth*.

Only the church at Ephesus was able to withstand the deceptive teachings of false apostles. Of them, Jesus said: "I know your works, and your labor, and your endurance, and that you cannot bear those who are evil; and that **you did test those who proclaim themselves to be apostles, but are not, and did find them liars**" (Rev. 2:2). This is a direct reference to the so-called "early church fathers"—the founders of what would become Roman Catholicism!

Like the brethren in Ephesus, we are to *test and prove the teachings of ministers and pastors* who claim to bring us the doctrine of God! If we fail to recognize false teachers and their teachings, we will succumb to their soothing, but evil, influence and be seduced by the forces of spiritual darkness. The apostle John warned that we cannot have fellowship with God if we are walking in spiritual darkness. "And this is the message that we have heard from Him and are declaring to you; that God is light and there is no darkness at all in Him. **If we proclaim that we have fellowship with Him, but we are walking in the darkness, we are lying to ourselves, and we are not practicing the Truth**" (I John 1:5-6).

Only by walking in the light of the truth can we have fellowship with God the Father and Jesus Christ. Those who claim to know God *but do not practice the truth* are only deceiving themselves.

God Allows Deception and Apostasy—Even Within the Church!

Numerous passages in the New Testament describe the insidious deception that led the early church to apostatize from the truth. Apostasy is the *end result* of rejecting the true teachings of Christ and embracing the false doctrines of spiritual darkness. This degenerate spiritual condition develops when a church becomes spiritually lax and lethargic—when its pastors teach pablum, compromise and "costless Christianity."

Christians who have lost their love of the truth—and who fail to "prove all things" by the Word of God—can *easily* be deceived by counterfeit doctrines. Without realizing it, churchgoers exchange their love of God and their faith in His Word for a *false faith* in corruptible men and their organizations.

Such misplaced loyalty and obedience is actually a form of *idolatry*. The subservient obeisance demanded by arrogant ministers in some corporate church organizations has replaced the true love and worship of God. Such exalted leaders have placed themselves *between* the brethren and God. True to the Scriptures, these **false ministers have "an outward appearance of godliness," but are guilty of "denying the power of *true* godliness."** We are admonished to "turn away" from all such leaders (II Tim. 3:5).

On his journey back to Jerusalem, the apostle Paul personally warned the elders of Ephesus that deceivers would enter the church after he was gone. In a special meeting with them at Miletus, Paul also declared that even *some of them*, who had been ordained as *ministers* of Christ, would begin to subvert brethren in the church (Acts 20:28-30). Later, when Paul was in prison, he wrote a letter to warn the entire church in Ephesus about deceitful men who would attempt to lead them astray. "**Do not let anyone deceive you with vain words**; for because of these things the wrath of God is coming upon the sons of disobedience. Therefore, **do not be joint partakers with them**" (Eph. 5:6-7.)

Paul shows that these men were working *within* the church. They may have even been highly trusted by the congregation. But Paul was inspired by God to warn the brethren *not to partake of the errors* of these deceivers. Those who did not heed Paul's warning were led away from God into the darkness of apostasy.

Likewise, the apostle Peter condemned false teachers who stealthily do their evil work *within* the church. He warned, "But there were also false prophets among the people [in the Old Testament], as indeed **there will be false teachers among you** [from within your congregations], **who will stealthily introduce destructive heresies**, personally **denying the Lord who bought them**, and bringing swift destruction upon themselves.

"And many people will **follow as authoritative** their destructive ways; and because of them, the way of the truth will be blasphemed. Also, through insatiable greed they will with enticing messages exploit you for [personal and financial] gain…" (II Pet. 2:1-3).

Why were some of the early New Testament churches led into apostasy? Why did God not intervene to keep false teachers from subverting the brethren? Paul gives the answer in his first epistle to the Corinthians: "For it is necessary that heresies [brought by false teachers] be among you, **so that the ones who are approved may become manifest among you**" (I Cor. 11:19).

Paul clearly tells us that God *allows* false teachings to arise within churches in order to bring to light those who are truly serving Him—and those who are not. Christians who are well grounded in the Word of God will be able to *discern* false teachers and will reject them; no deceiver will be able to seduce believers who *honestly* and *diligently* study the Scriptures. But those who compromise with the truth will fall into apostasy.

In his letter to the Ephesians, Paul urged the brethren to grow in the knowledge of Christ and to resist false teachings. We are not to be like immature children "**tossed and carried about with every wind of doctrine**, by the sleight of men in cunning craftiness…. [Rather, we are to be] holding the truth in love, [so that we] may in all things grow up into Him Who is the Head [of the Church], even Christ" (Eph. 4:14-15).

The Apostasy is Coming—Will You be Deceived?

In his sobering letter to the church at Thessalonica, the apostle Paul gives a powerful warning that Satan's deceptive tactics would continue down through the centuries and would reach a *climax* in the last generation shortly before the return of Christ. He writes, "Now we beseech you, brethren, concerning the coming of our Lord Jesus Christ and our gathering together to Him, that you not be quickly shaken in mind, nor be troubled—neither by spirit, nor by word [a false teaching], nor by [a false] epistle, as if from us, saying that the day of Christ is present.

"*Do not let anyone deceive you by any means* because that day will not come unless **the apostasy shall come first**, and the man of sin shall be revealed—[the Antichrist] the son of perdition, the one who opposes and exalts himself above all that is called God, or that is an object of worship; so that he comes into the temple of God and sits down as God, proclaiming that he himself is God" (II Thess. 2:1-4).

The prophecies of the New Testament clearly show that this Antichrist will arise out of the world's extant political and religious system referred to in Scripture as the "mystery of lawlessness" (verse 7). Paul shows that Satan's efforts to mislead mankind will culminate in the end-time deceptive work of the Beast and False Prophet of Revelation 13, leading to a *great apostasy* or "falling away" from the truth among Christians.

Confirming what Paul wrote, Jesus gave the apostle John a startling vision (recorded in the book of Revelation) of the coming New World Order and of the Antichrist who will arise out of that system. John depicted this political system as a "beast" with "seven heads and ten horns" (Rev. 13:1-9). A second "beast"—*Satan's unified, worldwide religious system*—is described as having two horns "like a lamb." It speaks, however, "like a dragon" and performs "great wonders" (verses 11-13).

Those who fall prey to this final apostasy will *not* be duped suddenly. Rather, they will have exhibited a history of repeatedly compromising with the truth of God over time. Thus, the ultimate result of *deception* (however small or seemingly insignificant its beginning may be) is total apostasy—*the abandonment of one's faith* (the Greek literally means to push God aside. Apostasy is defined by *Webster's New World Dictionary* as "to abandon what one believes in").

In order to abandon the faith, one must have first been a *believer*. A person cannot abandon something he or she does not have. Being deceived is the *first step* toward apostasy. Apostasy is not the beginning of evil, it is the culmination of wave after wave of deception. This is why Paul emphatically warned, "**Do not let anyone deceive you by any means.**"

Paul's words are a timely warning for true Christians in these end times. The stage is now being set for the prophesied great apostasy—in the world's educational systems, in its governments, in the churches.

Many in the New Testament era failed to heed the warnings of Paul and the other apostles. Whole congregations gradually succumbed to the creeping "leaven" of false doctrine. The apostasy gained momentum after the death of Paul and Peter. John, the last of the original apostles, wrote his three epistles against the evils and subtleties of the developing apostasy, which was spearheaded by false teachers and false apostles. After his death, the churches of God were swept up in a sea of false doctrines. The end result was the rise of the Catholic Church!

Could You Fall for a One-World Religion?

Today, the knowledge of God is being pushed aside and eliminated. Basic moral values founded in God's Word, which the world had formerly accepted, are being systematically expunged or nullified in every aspect of life. In their place stands Satan's godless "New Age" human philosophy.

To fully control this apostasy, **Satan is bringing about the amalgamation of the world's religions into a united global church! It will become** *the new one-world religion.*

Indeed, forces are already conspiring to form this new global religion. According to a World Net Daily news report filed in 1999 by Jon Dougherty, representatives from the religious faiths of some 50 countries have held regular meetings since 1995 for the purpose of promoting one global religion (*Group Wants United Religion: Is Goal Mere Co-operation or Creation of One Faith?*; www.wnd.com/news/article.asp? ARTICLE_ID=15187; August 10, 1999).

Dougherty writes that a group known as the United Religions Initiative (URI) has sponsored numerous global events, six regional conferences and three global summits in San Francisco from 1996 to 1998—all aimed at "cooperation and peacemaking among religions and spiritual communities." URI officials typically use such buzzwords as "cooperation" and "peace" while denying that the organization exists for the purpose of forming a one-world religion. Dougherty is skeptical, however, noting that the URI refers to "forces in our world today that are calling for and supporting the creation of a *United Religions*"—a takeoff on the United Nations. The group is currently exploring what purpose, foundational values, principles, actions and organizational structure such a "UR" might eventually adopt.

Similar unification efforts are being made by the so-called "Parliament of the World's Religions" (www.parliamentofreligions.org). Supposedly, the group was created to "cultivate harmony among the world's religious and spiritual communities" with an eye toward, once again, "world peace." Since 1993, the organization has convened every five years in a major international city (Chicago, 1993; Cape Town, 1999; Barcelona, 2004; Melbourne, 2009).

While the "Parliament of the World's Religions" denies that it promotes a one-world religion, it proudly touts its "declaration towards a *global ethic.*" A "global ethic" is suspiciously close to a *global faith.* Like the URI, the group's terminology appears intentionally vague.

Working in concert with the URI and "Parliament of the World's Religions" is the International Religious Foundation (IRF). Using similar hazy rhetoric as the two previous groups, the IRF is "dedicated to world peace through religious dialogue and harmony" (from the Foundation's 1991 *World Scripture—A Comparative Anthology of Sacred Texts*, p. xiii). As a compilation of quotations from the religious texts of the world, the book purports to "honor the richness and universality of religious truth contained in the world's great scriptures" (p. xiii). Reading between the lines, **it is clear that the IRF shares the same ultimate goal,** *a global religion*—as "all religions are connected to the same Ultimate Reality [their politically-correct designation for God]" (p. 33; emphasis added).

According to the book's editor, Andrew Wilson, ecumenical efforts are at an all-time high. "A movement for wider ecumenism has begun, bringing together for dialogue leaders and scholars from all the world's religions" (p. 1). Wilson says that "as we move toward a world civilization"—a one-world government—there must be a "growing convergence and complementarity among faiths" (p. xi). He says all religions are to "inherit each other's spiritual foundation and prepare for mutual cooperation" (p. xiv).

Hesitant to use the phrase "one world religion," Wilson speaks of "the call [among scholars] for a *world theology*" (p. 2). He adds that "it is inadequate to treat [existing] religions as discrete and independent entities. We must [rather] seek new, *holistic* models [a global religion] to describe the human religious experience." And, "*World Scripture* can [be utilized to] *support a world theology* [can be used as "scripture" for a global religion] and guide us toward a unity of the world's peoples" (p. 3).

Even as recently as November of 2010, unconventional Muslim clerics orchestrated a "World Day of God" in which literally *all religions* were to participate in a day of prayer to "God" *as defined* by each particular faith. The event reeked of New Age pantheism mixed with dominant Islamic overtones (see www.IslamicSolutions.com).

Western critics of one-world-religion movements note that such efforts tend to **homogenize all religions in a meaningless amalgamation**. Indeed, **such "melting pot" religions ultimately *deny* the one true Creator God and Jesus Christ—preferring instead to relate to an ambiguous "Ultimate Reality**."

In a world long devoid of God's truth, this new fusion of religions will be received as a wonderful "spiritual advancement." In reality, it will be a grand pantheon of Satan's religions and his gods. This "new" union of all religions will be the prophesied "MYSTERY, BABYLON THE GREAT, THE MOTHER OF HARLOTS AND OF THE ABOMINATIONS OF THE EARTH" (Rev. 17:5). Just as Satan is inspiring an *ecumenical movement* among the religions of the world, he is also subverting all nations and governments into accepting a one-world government. This one-world government will be the Beast System which "Babylon the Great"—in the person of the great False Prophet—will ride (Rev. 13; 17:1-6).

Indeed, Satan's *final and greatest deception* is rapidly developing. Once reaching its zenith of satanic power, it will sweep all peoples and nations into blatant Satan worship—replete with false signs, miracles and lying wonders—all designed to usher in the Antichrist. Empowered by Satan himself, the False Prophet will call down fire from heaven, proclaiming the Antichrist as the savior of the world. With the exception of *true* Christians who have the Holy Spirit of God, **all the world will be utterly deceived** into believing that the Antichrist is indeed the manifestation of God in the flesh—the long-awaited Messiah.

People will have been prepared well in advance to accept and believe such lies. When the final Great Apostasy nears its climax and the greatest lies are taught, people of all nations will accept them with open minds. That grand deception is *just around the corner!* The final deception will be a one-world government with a one-world religion—one great Baby-lonian governmental and religious system set up in rebellion against God. This world-wide deception will be the greatest apostasy ever perpetuated! The grand finale of Satan's deception will be the "mark of the Beast," ac-companied by open worship and adoration of Satan as God. All those who refuse to worship Satan and the Beast will be sentenced to die (Rev. 13). Satan's *grand deception* will be so powerful and so compelling that the ar-mies of the world will literally fight against Jesus Christ when He returns (Rev. 16:13-16; 19:11-19).

Christianity Now Facing Wholesale Apostasy

As the prophesied apostasy is unfolding around the world, a spiritual apostasy—having been long in the making—has taken root within Christi-anity. Satan's goal is to destroy the truth of God and, if it were possible, de-stroy the *spiritual* Church of God! He aims to deceive and destroy every be-gotten son of God by any means possible. Since he cannot kill every true Christian physically, he uses his seductive deceptions to subvert and destroy them spiritually. **The most effective and least detectable method that Sa-tan uses to deceive true believers is the promulgation of false doctrines from *within* their own church organizations**.

This departure from the truth of God takes place gradually and sub-tly. One by one, false doctrines creep in and begin to replace the true teach-ings of God's Word. Little by little, the apostasy within "Churchanity" has taken hold, and truth and faith are being abandoned. Just as "a little leaven leavens the whole lump," so the acceptance of false doctrine acts as *spiritual leaven*—leavening whole congregations.

In baking, the leavening process begins slowly and imperceptibly as the tiny amount of leaven works its way throughout the large lump of dough. But once the leaven has permeated the entire lump, its pervasive ef-fect is clearly visible, as it completely leavens the whole lump. The original lump of dough is *completely changed* into a wholly leavened loaf of bread.

Spiritual leaven works the same way. When a little leaven of false doctrine enters a church, it must immediately be rejected. If it is allowed to remain, it will only grow and lead to the spread of error. Slowly and insidi-ously, more and more false doctrine will be introduced, until these deceptive teachings permeate the entire church. Such spiritual leaven can mushroom into mammoth doctrinal changes, completely transforming a church so that it no longer resembles a genuine church of Christ.

Paul also warned the Colossians, exhorting them not to allow any man to deceive or corrupt them with clever-sounding doctrines of philoso-phy. "Now this I say so that **no one may deceive you** by persuasive speech.... **Be on guard so that no one takes you captive** [as one stalks an animal to kill] **through philosophy and vain deceit, according to the tra-ditions of men**, according to the elements of the world, and not according to Christ" (Col. 2:4, 8). Peter admonished, "Be sober! Be vigilant! For your adversary the devil is prowling about as a roaring lion, seeking anyone he may devour. Whom **resist, steadfast in the faith**, knowing that the same afflictions are being fulfilled among your brethren who are in the world" (I Pet. 5:8-9).

Those who desire to follow the true teachings of Jesus Christ must constantly be on guard against Satan and his seductive teachings through false ministers. Every believer must heed the urgent warnings recorded in the New Testament. These inspired words were written for *all true Christians*, "on whom the ends of the ages are coming" (I Cor. 10:11). As true Christians, each of us has a personal responsibility to God—WE ARE NOT TO ALLOW ANYONE TO DECEIVE US BY ANY MEANS!

Those Who Do not Love the Truth Will be Judged

When people do not the love the truth of God, God gives them over to apostasy—to believing lies. People who turn to falsehoods believe them with the same conviction and intensity with which they formerly believed the truth. When that happens, they have surrendered themselves to Satan's deception! They are his captives! That is exactly what Satan wants—to delude them into accepting false doctrines so that he can ensnare them in his ultimate deception.

Those who turn away from the true teachings of God's Word and blindly follow false teachers will ultimately fall prey to Satan's most masterful deception—the end time *Great Apostasy*, led by the coming Antichrist, empowered by Satan with lying wonders! At that time, many so-called "Christians" who have *never loved the truth* will be so deluded that they will join the deceived masses of the world in their worship of Satan! Satan, who has deceived the whole world with his lies, will be welcomed with open arms and "worshipped as God" in the final delusion of the Great Apostasy (Rev. 13:4).

Only by loving the truth and *holding fast* to the true teachings of God's Word can we hope to escape this rapidly-developing, diabolical apostasy. Paul declared, "For the [Satanic] mystery of lawlessness is already working…. And then the lawless one [the Antichrist possessed by Satan himself] will be revealed (whom the Lord will consume with the breath of His mouth, and will destroy with the brightness of His coming).

"Even the one whose coming is according to the inner workings of Satan, with all power and signs and lying wonders, and with **all deceivableness of unrighteousness** in those who are perishing, **because they did not receive the love of the truth**, so that they might be saved.

"And for this cause, God will send upon them a powerful deception that will cause them to believe the lie, so that **all may be judged who did not believe the truth**, but who took pleasure in unrighteousness" (II Thess. 2:7-12).

Paul clearly states that those who *do not love the truth* will be judged because they delight in unrighteousness. They do not delight in keeping the commandments of God, which are righteousness (Psa. 119:172). That is why they turn to false doctrines. They want "smooth things," pablum, a carnal-friendly "Christianity"—to be free to live *immorally*, yet hide their unrighteousness with the *appearance* of godliness by attending church each week!

Paul foresaw a time when many in the church would slip into moral decadence. They would begin to delight in unrighteousness and would turn from the truth, *rejecting sound doctrine.* "For there shall come a time when they will not tolerate sound doctrine; but **according to their own lusts**"— their desire for "smooth things," pablum, a "costless Christianity"—"they shall accumulate to themselves a *great number of teachers*, having ears itching *to hear what satisfies their cravings*; and they shall *turn away* their own ears from the truth; and they shall be turned aside unto [religious] myths" (II Tim. 4:3-4).

Have you turned away your ears from hearing the truth? Are you rejecting sound doctrine? Have you accepted false doctrines of religious mythology as truth? What about the doctrine of the Trinity and the denial of the human nature of Jesus? Do you realize that the Trinity teaching attempts to change the very nature of God in order to conform to pagan philosophical ideas? Are these false doctrines being preached by ministers and teachers in *your* church? What about Easter, Christmas and Halloween? What about Sunday observance itself—which is a pagan counterfeit of the biblical seventh-day Sabbath? Many today *know* about the true Sabbath but refuse to observe the day because to do so would conflict with so many social activities—which are typically held on Saturday. How about you?

Mark this well—**all who turn away from the truth and embrace religious myths and religious holidays of pagan origin will end up in spiritual blindness and will ultimately fall into apostasy**.

The Bible teaches us that when the leaders of any church organization reject the truth, they are judging God's Word as unworthy of their acceptance and belief. In judging God, they have usurped the prerogatives of God, just as Adam and Eve did in taking of the forbidden tree. They have cut themselves off from God and have become blind leaders of the blind. If such ministers and leaders continue unrepentant in their errors, God's judgment is sure to follow! After a period of warning, which God always allows, He will execute His judgment against them and their organizations— ministers as well as members. The apostle Peter wrote, "For the time has come **for judgment to begin with the household of God**; and if it first begins with us, what will be the end of those who do not obey the gospel of God?" (I Pet. 4:17).

Judgment is sure to come upon every churchgoer and every minister who turns aside from the truth and follows after religious myths. But God tells us in His Word that He desires mercy and not judgment! Anyone who truly repents before God will have his or her sins placed under the blood of Jesus Christ and will find mercy. But if there is no repentance after repeated warnings, then judgment will follow—for God will not be mocked! Those who forsake righteousness and follow after unrighteousness will reap the reward of unrighteousness! "Do not be deceived. God is not mocked; for whatever a man sows, that shall he also reap. For the one who sows to his own flesh shall reap corruption from the flesh. But the one who sows to the Spirit shall reap eternal life from the Spirit" (Gal. 6:7-8).

It is God's desire that all true Christians sow of the Spirit to eternal life. We are to grow in godly character, to exemplify the *love of God* in our lives so that we may bear the fruits of the Spirit, which are "love, joy, peace, long-suffering, kindness, goodness, faith, meekness, self-control" (Gal. 5:22-23). Only then can we reap the reward of eternal life.

CONCLUSION

Lord, *Now* What Should I Do?

As a whole, modern-day institutional "Christianity" has *failed* to meet the spiritual needs of its members. Rather than being a sanctuary for the personal growth and development of its followers, "Churchanity" seems narrowly fixated on image, "public relations" and membership drives. Corruption, politics and abuse continue to plague corporate church structures, while congregations are slowly but steadily consumed by worldliness. Having lost touch with the real-life issues churchgoers are facing, pastors and church leaders seem oblivious to the reality that so-called Christians today are *no different* than unbelievers.

Indeed, **Christianity is rapidly spawning a new generation of** *plastic* **Christians—those whose belief in Jesus amounts to nothing more than a get-out-of-hell-free card**. As David Kupelian quips, "Christianity has been dumbed down into a bumper-sticker religion" (*The Marketing of Evil*, p. 235). "This dumbed-down version of Christianity doesn't require honest introspection or courage or self-denial or patience. The only ingredient it needs is a guilty person who's sick of feeling guilty, wants relief, wants to feel better about himself, and desires an 'insurance policy' to keep him out of hell. But even the most insincere person wants to feel better about himself, wants relief from guilt, and fears death..." (p. 239).

The inevitable result of such an approach is a *counterfeit* **religious experience—***false conversion*. Interestingly, Christian writers are always talking about the "churched" and the "unchurched"—but not about the *converted* and the *unconverted*. Do you know what "conversion" really means? Is your Christian experience genuine—or is it a "knockoff"? Being merely "churched" does not mean that one is truly *converted*—for conversion (Acts 3:19; etc.) entails *repentance* and genuine *change* (see Appendix A, "Who and What Is a True Christian?"). As Kupelian notes, the "trivialization of Christianity into a mantra of belief—but separated from works, from obedience to God's laws, and even more fundamentally, separated from basic honesty, integrity, love of truth and *true repentance*—has **ushered in a generation of shallow, ineffectual and invisible Christians**" (p. 239; emphasis added).

But those of genuine faith realize that true Christianity is a lifelong *uphill battle* that only the few are willing to undertake: "Enter in through the **narrow gate**; for wide is the gate and broad is the way that leads to destruction, and many are those who enter through it; **for narrow is the gate and difficult is the way that leads to life, and few are those who find it**" (Matt. 7:13-14).

Are *you* one of those few who are willing to *find* the "narrow gate"—to strive diligently to enter into the Kingdom of God? Like an increasing number of American churchgoers, perhaps *you* too can personally identify with the problems extant in mainstream Christianity; perhaps you already consider yourself to be among the rapidly-growing group of church-goers who are ready to look elsewhere—to look *outside* the established corporate church for the spiritual inspiration, teaching and guidance you need.

In the year 2000, according to George Barna's research, 70 percent of Americans experienced and expressed their faith through traditional church attendance; only *five* percent did so in an *alternative environment*—small groups, home churches, coffee-house meetings, etc. But based on trends already well under way, Barna expects the number of those seeking a non-traditional spiritual experience to rise by 2025 to *30 percent* (with a corresponding drop in traditional church attendance) (*Revolution,* p. 49).

Barna writes that **such alternative means of finding spiritual fulfillment are the direct result of "extreme frustration or disillusionment" at the "relatively compromised and complacent state of faith in the nation today"** (pp. 39, 49; emphasis added). He also notes that "the churches that have suffered most are those who stuck with the one-size-fits-all approach, typically proving that one-size-fits-nobody" (p. 63). Barna says he spent years searching for evidence that God was transforming lives through churches; in the end, he was mostly disappointed at how relatively rare such instances were. Eventually, however, his research revealed that such transformations were indeed taking place—but through ministries operating *outside* of the local church (p. 53).

Dubbed spiritual "mini-movements," such alternative groups include home churches, small-group studies, marketplace (coffeehouse) groups—even homeschooling groups. A key facet of the alternative spiritual mini-movement is that **"millions of people who are growing as Christians and passionate about their faith have come to recognize that the local church is not—and need not be—the epicenter of their spiritual adventure"** (Barna, p. 58). Typically, those interested in non-traditional fellowships are looking to address previously unmet spiritual needs through "customized experiences" relevant to the key issues of daily life (p. 62). He writes, "the fastest-growing macro-models of church are the house church and the cyber-church formations" (p. 65).

Some Practical Suggestions

Are you ready to venture *outside* of the established church—to find genuine spirituality in an alternative type of fellowship? Are you ready to take a stand for the *truth,* for *real Christianity*—even if it means forsaking traditional church attendance?

If so, here are some helpful recommendations:

1) **Realize that *you*—and others like you—*are the church*.** Jesus said, "I will build My church" (Matt. 16:18). And He did—but it isn't made

of bricks and mortar; it isn't identified by corporate organizations or hierarchies of men. The true church of God is made up of those who are genuinely called of God (John 6:44)—those who have been immersed *into* the body of Christ through conversion, baptism and the receipt of the Holy Spirit (Acts 2:38). The church Jesus founded *originally* met in homes (Rom. 16:5; I Cor. 16:19; Col. 4:15), where small numbers of believers "gathered in His name" (see Matt. 18:20). Do not let anyone mislead you into believing that you *must* attend an organized church. If the church you have traditionally attended does not reflect the truth of genuine Christianity *in every way*, it is time for you to look elsewhere. Do not continue to associate with any church that teaches contrary to the Scriptures or where the fruit of God's Spirit is lacking.

2) Whatever alternative form of spiritual fellowship you *join* or *initiate*, **start fresh by turning to God in heartfelt *repentance* of any wrong beliefs and practices** you may have learned in your former church. Look to God the Father and Jesus Christ as you diligently study the pure Word of God to "prove all things" (I Thess. 5:21).

3) Throughout this book, we have emphasized the importance of keeping God's *commanded* seventh-day Sabbath holy, which is Saturday. Remember this: **diligent Sabbath-keeping is a vital *key* to a genuine relationship with God**. If you expect God to bless your life spiritually—and to bless your new home-study group or fellowship—you must *honor as holy* the day He made holy (for more information on Sabbath-keeping, see the recommended Web sites below).

4) In time, some may be desirous of baptism (or, perhaps, concerned about the validity of their previous baptism). Baptism—which represents one's spiritual covenant with God—is a momentous step for the believer and requires careful spiritual preparation. Please feel free to contact us for counsel and assistance (contact information is available on our Web sites below).

5) **Don't let your new "house church" become a social club**. Meeting in homes creates an informal atmosphere, which is fine to a point. But keep it organized and on target—or it will become just another feel-good social gathering with little spiritual value. Hundreds of small, home-based groups are forming across the country, but many of them are perpetuating the *same* mistakes and false teachings found in the corporate churches. Remember *why* you left organized Christianity!

6) It is inevitable that someone will assume a "leading" role within the group. But that person should not be allowed to "lord over" fellow believers (Mark 10:42-43). Do not repeat past mistakes of allowing any *man* to stand between you and God—Jesus Christ alone is our mediator!

7) **There will be a need for those *qualified* in teaching in the Word of God**. In her book *Quitting Church*, Duin notes that one of the problems with house churches is that small-group leaders typically have little training in teaching. She asks, "How is the emerging house-church

movement going to be any different [from corporate churches] without qualified leadership?" (p. 66). This presents a real problem for those seeking Bible-centered fellowship outside of the traditional church setting.

One practical solution is to rely on educational materials produced by various ministries operating via the Internet. But again, the same warnings apply: be diligent to "prove all things"—be sure materials are truly biblical. *The danger of false teachings propagated through so-called Christian Web sites is very real!* As a group or fellowship, work together to thoroughly check up on *any* Web-based support ministry.

The Internet site **www.churchathome.org** is dedicated to providing small, home-based fellowship groups with quality *scripturally-based* materials and resources necessary for a solid Christian foundation. Designed especially for those who are seeking genuine spirituality outside of the corporate church environment, the "Church at Home" site features over one hundred 30-minute video presentations on various topics; the videos can be viewed "live" or downloaded for later use. The most helpful **video titles** include:

- Who is God?

- The Kingdom of God

- God, How Do I Find You?

- How Did Mankind Get A Sinful Nature?

- What is Sin?

- How the Christian World Has Been Deceived

- Which Day is the True Christian Sabbath?

- The Love of God and the Law of God

- Quitting Church

"Church at Home" also features numerous **downloadable articles** on a variety of biblical topics. Here are a few sample titles:

- A Call to Repentance

- The Biblical Truth About Sabbath-Keeping

- Christ Was Taught Directly by God the Father

- Did Christ's Sacrifice Bring an End to the Law?

Conclusion

- Did Jesus Abolish the Seventh-day Sabbath?

- Did the Apostle Paul Teach Against the Laws and Commandments of God?

- The Four Great Love Commandments

- Have the Ten Commandments Been Nailed to the Cross?

- How Did Jesus Christ Fulfill the Law and the Prophets?

- How to Study the Bible

- It's God—Not the Economy or Politics

- Jesus Christ—Lord God of the Old Testament and Son of God

- Jesus Christ—Spiritual Lawgiver

- "Learn Not the Way of the Heathen"

- One Perfect Sacrifice

- Ninety Facts About God

- What does it Mean to be Born Again?

- What Happens to the Dead?

- What is the Purpose of the New Testament?

- Whatever Happened to Moral Absolutes?

- When and How Will Jesus Christ Return to the Earth?

- Who Will Save You?

For more intensive and advanced study materials, "Church at Home" has a sister site, **www.cbcg.org**. With a theme of *Restoring Original Christianity—For Today!*, this site features over 1500 audio sermons and Bible studies, including hundreds of video sermons, sermon transcripts and biblical articles—all available for download free of charge.

To get you started, we recommend you request the **Introductory Study Package No. 1**—which includes the following booklets:

- Fourteen Rules for Bible Study (also included in the back of this book)

- How Did Jesus Christ Fulfill the Law and the Prophets?

- Is God a Trinity?

- The Mystery of the Trinity

- The Truth About Christmas

- When was Jesus Born?

Also be sure to request the following from www.cbcg.org:

- The Grace of God (booklet)

- The Holy Sabbath (sermon series)
  www.cbcg.org/holy_sabbath.htm

- Refuting Sunday-keeping (sermon series)
  www.cbcg.org/refuting_sunday_keeping.htm

Because the diligent study of the Scriptures is such a vital part of your Christian life, be sure to visit the site **www.restoringtheoriginalbible.com** to learn about *The Holy Bible In Its Original Order*—a new, easy-to-read translation in which the books are arranged in their correct manuscript order.

As you step out in faith to either form a new home-based fellowship or join an existing "house church," strive to keep God at the center of your efforts. Pay special attention to honoring and obeying Him *in everything*; worship Him *in spirit* and *in truth* and He will indeed bless you with peace of mind and genuine spiritual growth!

Appendices

APPENDIX A

Who and What Is a True Christian?

The world has various ideas about who and what a "Christian" is or isn't. Some think a Christian is anyone born into a Christian-professing family and christened by a priest or minister. Others say a Christian is one who has "given his heart to the Lord" and is "born again"—or perhaps one who simply **claims** to be a Christian.

Is it possible, however, for someone to live and die **assuming** that he or she is a Christian—only to find out in the Judgment that God **never recognized their brand** of "Christianity"? Christ, in fact, warned of that very possibility in Matthew 7:21-23.

What truly makes a person a Christian? How does GOD describe a Christian in His inspired word—the Bible?

Serious followers of Christ will diligently study their Bibles to understand the true definition of a Christian—and to make sure that they are, indeed, true Christians (II Tim. 3:15-17). They will have their minds and hearts set to love God the Father and Jesus Christ with all their hearts and all their minds and all their strength (Mark 12:28-30). They will be committed to **live by every word of God** (Matt. 4:4; Luke 4:4; Deut. 8:3), proving all things from the Scriptures (I Thess. 5:21; Acts 17:10-12).

No Longer Under the Penalty of Sin

Crucial to understanding the **Bible definition** of a Christian is the fact that all human beings have been sinners, including ourselves (Rom. 3:23). The penalty for sin is permanent death (Rom. 6:23). A Christian is one who has come to realize that he or she had been under that death penalty and in need of a Savior. A Christian understands that Jesus Christ **paid that penalty** by dying on the cross when He was completely innocent of any sin (II Cor. 5:21; I John 2:2; 4:10; Rev. 1:5; 5:9).

A Christian learns just **what, specifically, is sin**—and what brought the death penalty upon them in the first place. Again, the world has its own ideas about what sin is or isn't, but the Bible defines sin for us as the **transgression of the law** of God (I John 3:4).

A true Christian, then, is one who has had the blood of Jesus Christ's sacrificial death applied to him or to her—but only after having acknowledged and **repented** of their sins (toward God the Father) and accepted Christ as their personal Savior (Acts 3:19; 2:38; Ezek. 18:21-23). Repentance literally means a change of mind and attitude, as well as a complete **change of conduct.** In repentance, one literally **turns from** the way of sin (breaking God's law) that leads to death (Prov. 14:12; 16:25; Matt. 7:13) and begins walking God's way—the true, Christian **way of life** (John 14:4-6; Acts 16:17; 18:25-26; I John 2:3-6).

Living in God's Grace

In order to become a Christian one has to be baptized, by full water immersion, into the name of the Father, the Son and the Holy Spirit. After the laying on of hands (Heb. 6:2), the new convert receives the gift of the Holy Spirit from Christ and the Father, by which a person is begotten as a new creation in Jesus Christ (Mark 1:8; Acts 2:38; 8:14-17; II Cor. 1:22; I John 3:9, 22-24).

By simply believing in Jesus Christ and in His name, repenting of sin, and asking God the Father's forgiveness, one comes under God's saving **grace** (Rom. 3:23-26; 6:23). This grace (which is so precious!) is a **free gift** from God—totally undeserved by anyone. No amount of effort by anyone could ever come close to earning this gift of God's favor. Being a "good person" will not earn you salvation—for God does not "owe" salvation to anyone! "For by grace you have been saved through faith, and this *especially* is not of your own selves; *it is* the gift of God" (Eph. 2:8-9).

Once baptized—and having received the gift of God's Holy Spirit—what should the newly converted Christian then do? Can a true Christian continue living as before? Does being "under grace" mean that one can go back and continue practicing what he or she supposedly repented of? Absolutely not! The apostle Paul makes it clear that one is not to continue to **live in sin**—continually transgressing the laws and commandments of God. Notice Romans 6:1-3: "What then shall we say? **Shall we continue in sin, so that grace may abound**? MAY IT NEVER BE! We who died to sin, how shall we live any longer therein? Or are you ignorant that we, as many as were baptized into Christ Jesus, were baptized into His death?"

A New Life in Christ

Notice how Paul goes on in Romans Six to describe the **new life** of a true Christian. "Therefore, we were buried with Him through the baptism into the death; so that, just as Christ was raised from *the* dead by the glory of the Father, in the same way, we also should **walk in newness of life**. For if we have been conjoined together in the likeness of His death, so also shall we be *in the likeness* of *His* resurrection. Knowing this, that our old man was co-crucified with *Him* in order that the body of sin might be destroyed, so that we might no longer be enslaved to sin; because the one who has died *to sin* has been justified from sin. Now if we died together with Christ, we believe that we shall also live with Him, knowing that Christ, having been raised from *the* dead, dies no more; death no longer has any dominion over Him. For when He died, He died unto sin once for all; but in that He lives, He lives unto God. In the same way also, you should indeed reckon yourselves to be **dead to sin, but alive to God** through Christ Jesus our Lord. Therefore, do not let sin rule in your mortal body by obeying it in the lusts thereof. Likewise, do not yield your members as instruments of unrighteousness to sin; rather, yield yourselves to God as those who are alive from *the* dead, and your members *as* instruments of righteousness to

God" (Rom. 6:4-13, emphasis added).

In both the parable of the pounds (Luke 19:11-27) and the parable of the talents (Matt. 25:14-30), Christ makes it clear that once having received a gift from God, one is not expected to sit on it or bury it—but to **build on it**, to increase it. Christians are to grow spiritually to become ever more like Jesus and the Father (II Pet. 1:3-11; 3:18; Eph. 4:11-13; 5:1). With this goal in mind, the true Christian studies his or her Bible regularly (II Tim. 2:15) to learn to **follow the example** set by Christ when He walked the earth in the flesh (John 13:15; 14:6; I Pet. 2:21; I John 2:6). In this way, God leads one through the power of His Holy Spirit and creates in each Christian His godly character (Eph. 2:10) and the mind of Christ (Phil. 2:5).

Christ's Example Shows the Way

What was the example Jesus Christ set for His followers? For starters, He perfectly kept His Father's commandments (John 15:10). His life's example, however, was not merely a legalistic, letter-of-the-law obedience—it was obedience from the heart, because He loved the Father with his **whole being**. A true Christian is to love God the Father and Jesus Christ with all his heart, all his mind, all his soul, and all his strength—which is the greatest commandment of all (Matt. 22:37-40). In this passage Jesus declares that LOVE, whether toward God or neighbor, is the basis for all of God's spiritual law. Each precept of the law merely tells us **how to love**. Also, there is a **spirit and intent** behind every law or command of God— and that intent is best summed up in one word, LOVE. If God tells us to do (or not to do) something, His motivation is always love (I John 4:8).

In the Sermon on the Mount (Matt. 5, 6, 7), Christ outlined how the spirit and intent of the law translates into personal conduct. Belief in the principles He has taught, however, is not enough—for they are of value only IF one **applies and lives by them** (Matt. 7:24-27). A true Christian—who loves God and knows that His laws are based on love—will in faith obey from the heart whatever He asks of him or her (John 14:15; I John 5:3). And a Christian's obedience will not be based on fear (of losing salvation, etc.), or because it "earns" them anything—but will be motivated by their love toward God, and because they understand that heartfelt obedience empowers them to become more and more like God the Father and Jesus Christ.

Many, unfortunately, mistakenly think that love and obedience to God's commandments are somehow opposites—in conflict with one another. Nothing could be further from the truth! Often, those who claim to be Christian will say they "love the Lord" or "know the Lord"—yet they fail to obey Him. The apostle John has an answer for such people. "And by this *standard* we know that we know Him: if we keep [obey] His commandments. The one who says, 'I know Him,' and does not keep [obey] His commandments, is a liar, and the truth is not in him. On the other hand, *if* anyone is keeping [obeying] His Word, truly in this one the love of God is being perfected. By this *means* we know that we are in Him. Anyone who claims to dwell in Him is obligating himself also to walk even as He Himself walked" (I John 2:3-6).

A Spirit-led Life

Many churchgoers assume they are already pretty good people. The apostle Paul, on the other hand—after relating how he also did that which was not right—said of himself, "O wretched man that I am!" (Rom. 7:14-24). Why did a holy apostle and man of God call himself "wretched"? Because he understood that his own human nature was not godly—and he was honest and humble enough to admit it. He likewise admitted that—even after conversion—his old carnal nature still led him to sin, for which he had to repent and ask forgiveness.

Notice his explanation of human nature in Romans 8:7-14: "Because the carnal mind [the mind of the unconverted] *is* enmity against God, for it is not subject to the law of God; neither indeed can it *be*. Now then, those who are in *the* flesh cannot please God. However, you are not in *the* flesh, but in *the* Spirit, if *the* Spirit of God is indeed dwelling within you. But if anyone does not have *the* Spirit of Christ, he does not belong to Him. Now if Christ *be* within you, the body *is* indeed dead because of sin; however, the Spirit *is* life because of righteousness. Now if the Spirit of Him Who raised Jesus from *the* dead is dwelling within you, He Who raised Christ from *the* dead will also quicken your mortal bodies because of His Spirit that dwells within you. So then, brethren, we are not debtors to the flesh, to live according to *the* flesh; because if you are living according to *the* flesh, you shall die; but if by *the* Spirit you are putting to death the deeds of the body, you shall live. For as many as **are led by *the* Spirit of God**, these are *the* sons of God" (emphasis added).

A true Christian is one who is **led by the Spirit of God**. In order to grow in that Spirit, which is needed to obey God and grow more like Him, a true Christian draws on the Holy Spirit through regular prayer and Bible study and occasional fasting. Christ taught His disciples to pray (Matt 6:5-15; Luke 18:1-14) and set an example by beginning each day with prayer (Mark 1:35). The Bible is the "God-breathed" words of God (II Tim. 3:16; I Pet. 1:11-12), and is also a powerful source of God's Spirit. Concerning the very words which He spoke, Christ said "they are spirit and they are life" (John 6:63). He also taught the right approach to fasting (Matt. 6:16-18).

One might ask, "How does **faith** fit into all of this?" In the 11th chapter of Hebrews (often called the "Faith Chapter"), we find example after example of those who **"by faith"** performed something that God had commanded. In each case, those faithful demonstrated their faith by obedience to God. Clearly, **faith and obedience go hand in hand** (Heb. 11:7-38; Rev. 14:12). To think they are somehow at odds with one another is a gross error. A true Christian's faith will **show in what he or she does** (James 2:17-18, 26). It was Abraham's **obedience** to God, by faith, that made him "the father of the faithful" (James 2:21-24). When Christ returns, He will bring His reward with Him and render to each person "according as his **work** shall be" (Rev. 22:12).

Finally, a true Christian will fellowship with others of like mind when possible—again following the example of Jesus Christ (Mark 1:21; Heb. 10:25). By fellowshiping with one another, Christians also fellowship with God (I John 1:3)—thus strengthening their relationship with God and growing in His Way. A true Christian **demonstrates his or her love** for one another by serving and giving materially to those in need (Matt. 25:31-46; I John 3:17, 18)—as well as by praying for and encouraging one another (James 5:16). All of these are expressions of the true love of God.

This, then, is the **Bible description of a true Christian**—one who, through God's grace, has turned from a life of sin and death to a life of love, obedience and the good works of faith as led and empowered by God's Holy Spirit.

APPENDIX B

Fourteen Rules for Bible Study

Spiritual Keys to Understanding the Word of God

There are definite spiritual *keys* to understanding the Scriptures. The primary key is continually remaining in a loving, faithful and obedient relationship with God. Jesus said, "If you love Me, keep the commandments—namely, My commandments" (John 14:15). Likewise, in the Psalms we find that those who keep the commandments of God will be *given understanding*: "The fear of the LORD is the beginning of wisdom: **a good understanding** have all those who do His commandments" (Psa. 111:10). This is the foundation to understanding the Word of God.

In order to understand doctrine, we must study the Bible "line upon line and precept upon precept." The prophet Isaiah writes: "Whom shall He teach knowledge? And whom shall He make to understand doctrine? *Those* who are weaned from the milk and drawn from the breasts [that is, fully grounded in the basics of the Word of God]. For **precept** *must be* **upon precept**, precept upon precept; **line upon line**, line upon line; **here a little, there a little**" (Isaiah 28:9-10). That is exactly how we need to study any scriptural question—look at *all* relevant passages on any given subject. The New Testament confirms this approach to understanding the Bible and establishing sound doctrine. The apostle Paul instructed Timothy: "Diligently *study* to show yourself approved unto God, a workman [in the Word of God] who does not *need to be* ashamed, rightly dividing [precept upon precept, and line upon line] the Word of the truth" (II Tim. 2:15).

The Word of God is called the Word of truth—and it is the Spirit of truth that teaches us all things. Jesus said, "But *when* the Comforter *comes*, *even* the Holy Spirit, which the Father will send in My name, that one **shall teach you all things**, and shall bring to your remembrance everything that I have told you" (John 14:26). This is a promise Jesus gave!

The Bible makes it clear that the Word of truth works together with the Spirit of truth to give understanding to those who love God and seek His will. It is self-evident that it is not possible for the carnal mind—which is deceitful above all things (Jer. 17:9)—to come to the knowledge of the truth of God. In fact, the carnal, unconverted mind is naturally *hostile* toward God and is not willing to be subject to God's laws (Rom. 8:7). Regardless of how brilliant or how great one's intellect may be, God's Word is not understood by human wisdom or reasoning. It is only through the Spirit of God that the Word of God can be understood.

Paul taught that spiritual truths can only be discerned and understood through the Spirit of God: "But God has **revealed *them* to us by His Spirit**, for the Spirit searches all things—even the deep things of God. For who among men understands the things of man except *by* the spirit of man which *is* in him? In the same way also, **the things of God no one understands except *by* the Spirit of God**. Now we have not received the spirit of the world, but the Spirit that *is* of God, so that we might know the things graciously given to us by God; which things we also speak, not in words taught by human wisdom, but in *words* taught by *the* Holy Spirit *in order to* communicate spiritual things by spiritual *means*. But *the* natural man does not receive the things of the Spirit of God; for they are foolishness to him, and he cannot understand *them* because **they are spiritually discerned**" (I Cor. 2:10-14).

Notice what Paul has to say about the profound value of studying the Scriptures: "And that from a child you have known the holy writings, which are **able to make you wise unto salvation** through faith, which *is* in Christ Jesus. All Scripture *is* God-breathed and *is* **profitable for doctrine**, for **conviction**, for **correction**, for **instruction in righteousness**; so that the man of God may be **complete**, **fully equipped** for every good work" (II Tim. 3:15-17).

The following "Fourteen Rules for Bible Study" outline how to "rightly divide" the Word of God. When these rules are followed, the student will find the truth of the Bible as revealed by the Spirit of truth. These rules are not designed to justify various doctrinal positions of men—but only the truth of God and the true doctrines of the Bible.

In addition to carefully examining the historical context of a particular passage of Scripture, students should refer to the original Hebrew and Greek in order to determine the precise meanings of key words. But one should never base doctrine solely on commentaries or other such "Bible helps." Doctrine must never be based on traditions of men—regardless of how knowledgeable or authoritative such men may appear.

Finally, we should all heed the apostle Peter's warning about allowing *personal* ideas and interpretations to cloud the truth of Scripture: "Knowing this first, that no prophecy of Scripture originated as anyone's own *private* interpretation; because prophecy was not brought at any time by human will, but the holy men of God spoke as they were moved by *the* Holy Spirit" (II Pet. 1:20-21).

Fourteen Rules for Bible Study

- Begin with Scriptures that are *easy* to understand

- Let the Bible interpret and prove the Bible. Don't look for what you *want* to prove—look for what the Bible *actually* says.

- Understand the *context*—the verses before and after, and the chapters before and after. Does your understanding of a particular verse harmonize with the rest of the Bible?

- As much as possible, try to understand the original Hebrew or Greek. But never try to establish doctrine or teachings by using only *Strong's Exhaustive Concordance of the Bible. Strong's* can be helpful at times, but is very limited.

- Ask: What does the Scripture *clearly say*?

- Ask: What does the Scripture *not* say?

- Ask: To whom was the book written?

- Ask: Who wrote it?

- Ask: Who said it?

- Understand the *historical time frame* in which the book was written.

- Base your study on the scriptural knowledge you already have. What do you *know* up to this point in time?

- Do not allow personal *assumptions* or *preconceived* ideas to influence your understanding and conclusions.

- Do not form conclusions based on *partial* facts, insufficient information, or the opinions and speculations of others.

- Opinions—regardless of how strongly you feel about them—don't necessarily count. Scripture *alone* must be your standard and guide.

APPENDIX C

Keys to Answered Prayer

Prayer is the most vital link between God and human beings. But there is much confusion on how to pray and how to have your prayers answered. Most religions, whether Christian or otherwise, feature some type of prayer. Many have forms of prayer where chants or a continual repeating of certain words are used. Sometimes "rosary" beads are devotedly utilized, where each bead is said to symbolize or represent something. People pray before idols, crucifixes, icons and pictures, hoping that these will somehow make their prayers more effective. In rare cases, people have been known to physically torture themselves in bizarre ceremonies, convinced that such bloody suffering is especially appealing to God.

In Judaism, pre-written prayers are recited at almost every occasion, and compulsory benedictions are uttered by devout Jews throughout the day. Prayer shawls are often worn in an attempt to appear more pious.

Oriental religions, such as in Tibet, have for centuries utilized prayer wheels. A prayer would first be written on a wheel; then, every time the wheel was spun, the prayer was supposedly sent up to heaven. (Similarly, we have computer programs today that can repeat user-specified prayers all day long.) Catholics and Buddhists use candles, wherein prayers are believed to drift up to heaven along with the smoke of the burning candle.

But such *ritualized* pagan prayers go no further than the spinning of the prayer wheel, the smoke of the candle, or the electronic repetition of a computer. God is not interested in chants, endlessly repeated phrases, or the superstitious fingering of beads. Such methods are *mechanical* and have nothing to do with true biblical prayer. **In fact, ritual prayers are evidence that we are just too busy to *really pray from our hearts*.**

The *truth* is that God does not want us to pray in any of these ways. The keys for truly sincere prayer that God will hear and answer are contained in the Bible, not in the precepts, superstitions, traditions or inventions of men.

How *Not* to Pray

Jesus Christ, in whose name all Christians are to pray, gave precise instructions on how *not* to pray. After clearly explaining that Christians are not to do their "alms" or religious works before others, to be seen of them, He continued, saying, "And when you pray, you shall not be as the hypocrites, for they love to pray standing in the synagogues and on the corners of the streets, in order that they may be seen by men. Truly I say to you, they have their reward.

"But you, when you pray, enter into a private room; and after shutting the door, **pray to your Father Who is in secret**; and your Father Who sees in secret shall reward you openly.

"And when you pray, **do not use vain repetitions**, as the heathen do; for they think that by multiplying their words they shall be heard. Now then, **do not be like them**; for your Father knows what things you have need of before you ask Him" (Matt. 6:5-8).

A vivid example of Christ's instructions is found in the encounter of Elijah the prophet with the prophets of Baal. In this case, the people of Israel were following Baal, the supposed sun god, but clung to the idea that they could worship the true God by using pagan methods. Notice Elijah's response: "And Elijah came to all the people and said, 'How long will you vacillate between two different opinions? If the LORD is God, follow Him. But if Baal is God, then follow him.' And the people did not answer him a word.

"And Elijah said to the people, 'I, I alone, remain a prophet of the LORD. But Baal's prophets are four hundred and fifty men. Now let them give us two bulls, and let them choose one bull for themselves, and cut it in pieces and lay it on wood. But place no fire under it. And I will dress the other bull and lay it on wood, and place no fire under it. And you call on the name of your gods, and I will call on the name of the LORD. And it shall be, the God that answers by fire, He is God.' And all the people answered and said, 'The word is good.'

"And Elijah said to the prophets of Baal, 'Choose one bull for yourselves, and prepare first, for you are many. And call on the name of your god, but place no fire under it.' So they took the bull which was given them, and they dressed it, and called on the name of Baal from morning even until noon, saying, 'O Baal, hear us.' But there was no voice, nor any who answered. Then they leaped upon the altar which was made.

"Now it came to pass at noon, Elijah mocked them and said, 'Cry aloud with a great voice, for he is a god. Either he is meditating, or he is pursuing, or he is in a journey. Perhaps he is asleep and must be awakened!' And they cried with a loud voice and cut themselves with knives and lances until the blood gushed out upon them.

"So it came to pass when midday was past, and when they prophesied until the offering of Elijah's oblation, there was neither voice, nor any to answer, nor anyone who paid attention" (I Kings 18:21-29).

Next, Elijah called all the people near, had the altar built, set the wood and dressed bullock in order. Then he had four barrels of water poured over the sacrifice, three times, until it was drenched and the trench around the altar was full of water.

When Elijah prayed, it was not long, loud or bloody from self-flagellation; rather, it was short and believing. He said, " 'LORD, the God of Abraham, Isaac, and of Israel, let it be known this day that You are God in Israel, and that I am Your servant, and that I have done all these things at

Your word. Hear me, O LORD, hear me, that this people may know that You are the LORD God, and that You have turned their heart back again.'

"Then the fire of the LORD fell and burned up the burnt sacrifice and the wood, and the stones and the dust, and licked up the water that was in the trench. And when all the people saw, they fell on their faces. And they said, 'The LORD, He is the God! The LORD, He is the God!' " (I Kings 18:36-39).

The same thing applies to us today. Do we really love, believe and have faith in the true God, or do we have a "religion" that is comfortable, allowing us to do anything we please. This account shows that God will hear and answer our prayers, and that *we need not pray like the heathen.*

Why Prayers Are Not Answered

In Isaiah 59 we find God's reasons why some prayers are not answered. "Behold, the LORD'S hand is not shortened that it cannot save, nor is His ear heavy that it cannot hear. But **your iniquities have come between you and your God**, and **your sins have hid His face from you**, that He will not hear, for your hands are defiled with blood, and your fingers with iniquity; your lips have spoken lies, your tongue has muttered perverseness. None calls for justice, nor does anyone plead for truth; they trust in vanity and speak lies. They conceive mischief and bring forth iniquity" (Isa. 59:1-4).

People claim to believe in God and peace, but the results of man's ways are death and mass destruction. Government leaders hold prayer breakfasts, religious masses and use the name of God as if He supports their efforts—while lying, corruption and stealing are the order of the day. Prayer is a controversial issue in public schools, while in too many schools sports, drugs, pleasures and immorality seem to be the major curriculum.

Many religious leaders legislate dogma and tradition as more important than God's Holy Word, thereby promoting humanly-devised practices learned by rote: "And the LORD said, 'Because this people **draw near Me with their mouth, and with their lips honor Me, but their worship of Me is made up of the traditions of men learned by rote**, and **their fear toward Me is taught by the commandments of men**; therefore, behold, I will proceed to do again a marvelous work among this people, even a marvelous work and a wonder, for the wisdom of their wise ones shall perish, and the wisdom of their intelligent ones shall vanish' " (Isa. 29:13-14).

All of these practices constitute sin. Sins and iniquities separate us from God and result in unanswered prayers. Most people do not know what sin is. Sin is the *breaking* of God's laws and commandments (I John 3:4)! The world's religions insist that God accepts their vain worship and vain prayers. But God detests such practices because *by using His name* they are making Him serve with their sins: "Yet you have not called upon Me, O Jacob; much less have you troubled yourself about Me, O Israel.... [But]

you have made Me serve with your sins; you have wearied Me with your iniquities. I, even I, am He who blots out your transgressions for My own sake, and will not remember your sins. Put Me in remembrance; let us plead together; declare yourself, that you may be justified" (Isa. 43:22, 24-26).

We Must Worship God in Spirit and Truth

God is Spirit and there is no need to worship Him with the aid of physical things. God is interested in the *attitude* and *intent of the heart* of a person—not idols, beads or hypnotic chants.

Here is what Jesus said about worshiping God. "But the hour is coming, and now is, when the true worshipers shall worship the Father **in spirit and in truth**; for the Father is indeed seeking those who worship Him in this manner. God is Spirit, and those who worship Him must worship **in spirit and in truth**" (John 4:23-24).

Jesus said that God's Word was *the truth* (John 17:17). So if we are to worship God in *spirit* and *truth*, we must worship Him and pray to Him according to the instructions in His Holy Word. This is actually an extension of loving God with all of one's heart, mind and being.

Eight *Keys* to Answered Prayer

Below are eight biblical keys to answered prayer. It is important that you look up and *study* each of the passages listed, proving the *truth* from the Word of God.

1) PRAY ACCORDING TO GOD'S WILL

Matt. 6:10	James 4:1-4	John 5:30
Dan. 3:16-18	I John 5:16-17	Luke 22:42

2) BELIEVE GOD AND WHAT HE SAYS IN HIS WORD

Heb. 3:12	Rom. 4:20-21	Mark 11:20-26
Matt. 8:5-13	James 1:5-7	Mark 9:14-29
James 2:5-26	Acts 17:11	

3) BE REPENTANT AND SEEK GOD FROM YOUR HEART

Isa. 1:15-20	Joel 2:12-14	II Chron. 15:2
Isa. 55:6-11	Acts 3:19	I John 1:6-10
Luke 18:9-14		

4) BE FERVENT AND ZEALOUS

James 5:16	Heb. 5:11-14	Luke 22:43-44
Hosea 7:14	Rev. 3:14-21	Eph. 6:18

5) HAVE GODLY FEAR AND HUMILITY

Psa. 111:10	Matt. 10:28	Heb. 4:1-16
Matt. 15:21-28	Luke 18:9-14	Isa. 66:1-2
I Pet. 5:5-10	James 4:6-10	

6) BE PERSISTENT AND NEVER GIVE UP

Luke 11:1-13	Luke 18:1-8	Eph. 6:18
Rom. 12:12	I Thess. 5:17	Col. 4:2-3
Col. 3:17	Phil. 4:6	

7) BE OBEDIENT TO GOD'S LAWS AND COMMANDMENTS

John 14:13-24	Rom. 6:16	John 15:1-17
I John 2:3-6	I John 3:4	I John 3:18-24
I John 5:1-3	Acts 5:32	I Pet. 1:14, 22
Prov. 15:8, 29	Prov. 28:9	I Pet. 2:1-2

8) PRAY TO GOD THE FATHER DIRECTLY IN CHRIST'S NAME

John 14:13-14	John 15:7, 16	John 16:23-27
Acts 4:12	Phil. 4:7-9	Rom. 8:9-39

The "Lord's Prayer"—An Outline Prayer

Many new believers ask, "How do I properly pray to God?" That's a fair question—even Jesus' disciples asked Him, "Lord, teach us to pray" (Luke 11:1). In response, Christ gave what could be called a *model prayer*—the so-called "Lord's prayer" found in Matthew 6:9-13 and Luke 11:1-4.

Contrary to popular opinion, the "Lord's prayer" is *not to be repeatedly recited*; rather, it was given by Jesus as a *teaching outline* of what one should cover when praying to God. Indeed, each phrase of Jesus' "model prayer" is instructive. (The true "Lord's prayer" is one He actually prayed—John 17. The entire chapter is the prayer Jesus prayed just before His arrest. Notice that even John 17 follows the outline Jesus gave in His "model prayer.")

If you will follow this model as a biblical *guideline*, your prayers will be answered. Always remember, "The sacrifice [or prayer] of the wicked is an abomination to the LORD, **but the prayer of the upright is His delight**.... The LORD is far from the wicked, but **He hears the prayer of the righteous**" (Prov. 15:8, 29).

• **Our Father Who is in heaven**. We are to pray to God, addressing Him as our loving Father. We are to acknowledge His supremacy over all the universe, and express thankfulness for His calling us into a personal relationship with Him and His Son. It is important that we approach God just as a child would approach his or her human father—with respect and admiration, *eager* to share our lives with Him, looking to Him as one Who looks after our every need.

On the night He was arrested, Jesus instructed the disciples to pray *directly to the Father*—not to Jesus Himself, or to the "Virgin Mary," or to any other supposed "saintly intermediary." Notice: "And in that day you shall ask Me nothing. **Truly, truly I tell you, whatever you shall ask the Father in My name, He will give you**. Until this day, you have asked nothing in My name. Ask, and you shall receive, that your joy may be full…. In that day, you shall ask in My name; and I do not tell you that I will beseech the Father for you, **for the Father Himself loves you**, because you have loved Me, and have believed that I came forth from God" (John 16:23-24, 26-27).

Jesus Christ is our high priest in heaven sitting at the right hand of God the Father to intercede for us. Paul writes that we are to approach God in humility, yet with boldness: "For the Word of God is living and powerful, and sharper than any two-edged sword, piercing even to the dividing asunder of both soul and spirit, and of both the joints and the marrow, and is able to discern the thoughts and intents of the heart. **And there is not a created thing that is not manifest in His sight; but all things are naked and laid bare before the eyes of Him to Whom we must give account**.

"Having therefore a great High Priest, Who has passed into the heavens, Jesus the Son of God, we should hold fast the confession of our faith. For we do not have a high priest who cannot empathize with our weaknesses, but one Who was tempted in all things according to the likeness of our own temptations; yet He was without sin. Therefore, **we should come with boldness to the throne of grace, so that we may receive mercy and find grace to help in time of need**" (Heb. 4:12-16).

• **Hallowed be Your name**. We are to honor God for His greatness, asking that His *name* be made "hallowed" or holy in all the earth. Ultimately, when the Kingdom of God is fully established over the earth by Jesus, the Father's name will be made holy in the minds and hearts of all mankind. It should be our innermost desire that all come to revere the holy name of God.

• **Your kingdom come**. We are to seek *first* the Kingdom of God (Matt. 6:33). Accordingly, we are to pray that God will soon establish His kingdom through Jesus' return to this earth. As we "sigh and cry" for the abominations of this world (Ezek. 9:4), we are to extol the greatness of that coming kingdom, talking with God in detail about how wonderful the age to come will be—contrasting it with the sorrows of this present age. This is a key element of our prayer life, as it reinforces our desire and longing for God's kingdom while emphasizing the need for us to prepare personally for that kingdom.

• **Your will be done, as in heaven, so also upon the earth**. Just as God's will is always done in heaven, we must seek for His will to be accomplished here on earth. Ultimately, this will be done through the establishment of His kingdom. Meanwhile, we must seek *His will* for our lives—asking Him to help us to understand what He wants for us and our loved ones. Our focus must not be on what we want, but on what God truly wants to accomplish in our lives as well as in the Church. We pray "Your will be done" knowing that God always has our best interest at heart (I Pet. 5:6-7). Importantly, as we pray for God's will to be accomplished, we must be ready and willing to *surrender to His will* in every area of our lives—repenting of any sin that stands contrary to His will.

• **Give us our bread as needed day by day**. As our loving Father, God wants us to look to Him for our physical and spiritual needs. He promises to care for us in every way (Matt. 6:25-34); but, to keep us from taking Him for granted, we still need to ask (Matt. 7:7-11). It is not wrong or selfish to discuss our *needs* with Him—so be specific. As long as we are asking according to His will, we may continue to patiently bring our needs before God (Luke 18:1-8). Above all, do not neglect to ask for daily strength and guidance—our *spiritual bread*. Also, ask that God will look after the needs of others.

• **And forgive us our sins, as we ourselves also forgive everyone who is indebted to us**. We must acknowledge that we still fall short and sin. Ask for God's forgiveness, confessing your specific sins. Thank God for Jesus' supreme sacrifice, acknowledging that it is through His shed blood that we have forgiveness and reconciliation. Ask God to strengthen you in these particular areas so you will not stumble and sin again—renewing your commitment to overcoming. Also, ask God to show you the areas of your life where you may be unknowingly sinning. Following David's example, use Psalm 51 as a guide in going before God in repentance of your sins.

A key aspect of asking for forgiveness is that we must *forgive others* of any and all offenses against us. God will not forgive us if we hold on to grudges or harbor anger against others. Ask God to help you to be forgiving.

• **And lead us not into [trial and testing], but rescue us from the evil one**. God does not tempt us with sin; we are tempted and led astray primarily by our own selfish desires (James 1:13-14). The point here is to pray that we will not *need* to be corrected through sore trials—and to ask God for guidance and strength in spiritually fighting against our enemy, Satan the devil (I Pet. 5:8). Again, be specific about the battles you face as you struggle to overcome your own nature, the world and Satan.

• **For Yours is the kingdom and the power and the glory forever. Amen**. Just as you begin by praising God for His greatness and glory, end your prayer by extolling His greatness, power and glory. With thanksgiving, be mindful again of His coming kingdom, His perfect will, and His awesome love for us. As instructed in John 14:13-14, we are to conclude our prayers by asking of the Father *in Jesus' name*. Indeed, it is through Christ that we are able to pray to the Father. Finally, the word "Amen" simply means "so be it."

Additional Points on Effective Prayer

• A "formal" tone is unnecessary and can hinder your prayers. Always be mindful of honoring God, but use a "conversational" tone—which will actually foster intimacy. God wants us to come to Him as a beloved parent. We should feel safe, confident, appreciated and loved in His presence. We are not to use repetitious "religious sounding" words or a syrupy tone with God—but entreat Him much like a child would his or her human father.

• Conversation with God is a two-way street. God *talks to us* as we read His Word—so never neglect Bible study.

• Prayer should be conducted *in private* (Matt. 6:6) when there will be minimal distractions.

• Don't "make time for prayer"—that's not really putting God first. Rather, build your day around your relationship with God, scheduling prayer *first*. Daily prayer will become a fixed habit over time—so stick with it.

• Value the opportunity through prayer to develop a strong, lifelong relationship with your spiritual Father. You must pray daily.

• God will not hear your prayers if you are living in sin. "Behold, the LORD'S hand is not shortened that it cannot save, nor is His ear heavy that it cannot hear. But **your iniquities have come between you and your God**, and **your sins have hid His face from you, that He will not hear**" (Isa. 59:1-2).

What kind of person will get God's attention? It really has nothing to do with where you "go to church" or where you fellowship; it has everything to do with your heart and mindset. "But to this one I will look, to him who is of a poor and contrite spirit and who trembles at My Word" (Isa. 66:2). Also, "the eyes of the Lord are on the righteous, and His ears are open to their supplications" (I Pet. 3:12).

• Never feel that God listens to some prayers while ignoring others. The apostle Peter said, "Of a truth I perceive that God is not a respecter of persons. But in every nation **the one who fears Him and works righteousness** is acceptable to Him" (Acts 10:34-35).

• **How often should you pray?** The apostle Paul wrote that we should pray without ceasing (I Thess. 5:17). Obviously, this does not mean we are to pray around the clock, but we are to make prayer a continual part of our daily life (this can also mean being in a continual *spirit of prayer* throughout the day). David said he prayed evening, morning and at noon (Psa. 55:17); when Daniel was going through a particularly difficult time, he prayed three times a day (Dan. 6:10). On some occasions Jesus started His day early, before daylight, to have extra time for prayer (Mark 1:35). Clearly, one should pray *more than once* each day.

• When you pray, *believe* that God hears and that He will respond. "But let him ask in faith, not doubting at all because the one who doubts is like a wave of the sea that is driven by the wind and tossed to and fro. Do not let that man expect that he will receive anything from the Lord" (James 1:6-7). Also, "all the things that you ask when you are praying, believe that you will receive them, and they shall be given to you" (Mark 11:24). "And this is the confidence that we have toward Him: that if we ask anything according to His will, He hears us" (I John 5:14).

• Again, God has *conditions* for answering prayer. "And whatever we may ask, we receive from Him **because we keep His commandments** and **practice those things that are pleasing in His sight**" (I John 3:22).

• Throughout the Bible, the example is to pray to God while on one's *knees*. You may pray silently, but you should also pray *aloud* at times.

• Utilize the book of Psalms in your prayers, as many of them are actually prayers. Read them aloud to God, adding your own thoughts or comments.

• Don't let prayer become a long list of what *you* want from God. Rather, spend considerable time **praying for the needs of others** (even your enemies). Properly focused prayer can help believers become more outgoing, selfless and concerned about others.

Also, be sure to download (or request) the sermon series *Keys to Answered Prayer* (www.cbcg.org/keys_answered_prayer.htm), and the sermon series *How to Pray* (www.cbcg.org/how_to_pray.htm).

Bibliography

Barkhuizen, Dr. Pieter. "Let the Truth Set Us Free," Biblical
    Research Perspectives; www.scribd.com/doc/22319905/Let-the-
    Truth-Set-Us-Free-052809

Barna, George. *Revolution*. Carol Stream, Ill.: Tyndale, 2005

Breen, Tom. "Congregations Struggle in Aging, Decaying
    Churches," The Associated Press, July 17, 2010

Chandler, Russell. *Understanding the New Age*. Dallas: Word
    Publishing, 2008

Chopra, Deepak. *The Third Jesus*. New York: Harmony, 2008

"Churchgoing in the UK." Tearfund Organization, 2007;
    www.whychurch.org.uk/trends.php

Dougherty, Jon. "Group Wants United Religion: Is Goal Mere
    Co-operation or Creation of One Faith?" *World Net Daily*, August
    10, 1999; www.wnd.com/news/article.asp?ARTICLE_ID=15187

Duin, Julia. *Quitting Church*. Grand Rapids: Baker Books, 2008

Dyck, Drew. "The 'Leavers': Young Doubters Exit the Church,"
    Christianity Today magazine's Web site; www.christianitytoday.
    com/ct/2010/november/27.40.html?start=1

Hurlbut, Jesse L. *The Story of the Christian Church*. Grand Rapids:
    Zondervan, 1980

Kinnaman, David. *UnChristian*. Grand Rapids: Baker Books, 2008

Kupelian, David. *The Marketing of Evil*. Nashville: WND Books,
    2005

Meacham, Jon. "The End of Christian America," *Newsweek
    Magazine*, April 13, 2009

Parliament of the World's Religions; www.parliamentofreligions.org

Tolle, Eckhart. *A New Earth—Awakening to Your Life's Purpose*. New York: Dutton, 2005

_____. *The Power of Now—A Guide to Spiritual Enlightenment*. Novato, Calif.: New World Library, 1999

Vul, Michelle. "Few Millennials Interested in Religion, Study Finds," *The Christian Post*, Jan. 12, 2011; www.christianpost.com/article/20110112/few-millenials-interested-in-religion-study-finds/

_____. "*Generation Ex-Christian* Uncovers Why People Leave the Faith," *The Christian Post*, Jan. 6, 2011; www.christianpost.com/article/20110106/generation-ex-christian-uncovers-why-people-leave-the-faith/

Waggoner, Brad. "LifeWay Surveys the Formerly Churched; Can the Church Close the Back Door?" www.lifewayresearch.com

Wilson, Andrew. *World Scripture—A Comparative Anthology of Sacred Texts*. St. Paul, Minn.: Paragon House, 1991

Wilson, Jared. *Your Jesus is Too Safe*. Grand Rapids: Kregel, 2009

World Day of God; www.IslamicSolutions.com